THE VILLAGE IS LIKE A WHEEL

The Village Is Like a Wheel

Rethinking Cargos, Family, and Ethnicity in Highland Mexico

ROGER MAGAZINE

THE UNIVERSITY OF
ARIZONA PRESS
TUCSON

THE UNIVERSITY OF ARIZONA PRESS

www.uapress.arizona.edu

Library of Congress Cataloging-in-Publication Data
Magazine, Roger, 1969–
    The village is like a wheel : rethinking cargos, family, and ethnicity in highland Mexico /
Roger Magazine.
        p. cm.
    Includes bibliographical references and index.
    ISBN 978-0-8165-1161-7 (cloth : alk. paper) 1. Indians of Mexico—Mexico—
Tepetlaoxtoc—History. 2. Indians of Mexico—Mexico—Tepetlaoxtoc—Social conditions.
3. Indians of Mexico—Mexico—Tepetlaoxtoc—Economic conditions. 4. Urban-rural
migration—Mexico—Tepetlaoxtoc. 5. Social change—Mexico—Tepetlaoxtoc.
6. Festivals—Mexico—Tepetlaoxtoc. 7. Cargo cults—Mexico—Tepetlaoxtoc.
8. Tepetlaoxtoc (Mexico)—Social conditions. 9. Tepetlaoxtoc (Mexico)—Rural
conditions. 10. Tepetlaoxtoc (Mexico)—Economic conditions. I. Title.
    F1219.1.T293M33 2012
    972'.46—dc23
                                                                    2012019380

Publication of this book is made possible in part by the proceeds of a permanent
endowment created with the assistance of a Challenge Grant from the National
Endowment for the Humanities, a federal agency.

For Matt and Criss

Contents

Illustrations

Acknowledgments

This book could not have been written without the financing for fieldwork research generously provided by the Dirección de Investigación of the Universidad Iberoamericana and the Consejo Nacional de Ciencia y Tecnología (CONACyT). I am also grateful to the University Iberoamericana for providing a year-long sabbatical leave during which I completed most of the writing.

Many people have contributed to this book's completion, and I wish to thank them all. Given the limited space, I can mention only a few by name. Carmen Bueno and Helena Varela created supportive work environments as department directors in different periods. I also wish to thank my colleague Marisol Pérez Lizaur for her support and the opportunity to exchange ideas on the Texcoco region. This book would have been inconceivable without the collaboration I have enjoyed with David Robichaux over the years. I am indebted to him for sharing his impeccable knowledge of Mesoamerican societies, for the encouragement he has provided, and for reading and commenting on earlier drafts. A number of graduate students at the Universidad Iberoamericana contributed important insights during discussions in seminars and through their research. I enjoyed and benefitted from the opportunity of working closely with a few of them on topics related to this book: Junior Encarnación Ruiz, Aki Kuromiya, Rubén Lechuga Paredes, Minerva López Millán, David Lorente, Martha Araceli Ramírez Sánchez, and Vera Regehr.

I am indebted to Elizabeth Ferry for commenting on earlier versions of the book and for the opportunity to present my ideas to her colleagues and students at Brandeis University. Casey Walsh patiently listened to my reckless formulation of ideas on various occasions. I wish to thank Johannes Neurath, John Monaghan, and James Taggart for their insights and collaboration on different occasions. Jacques Ramírez generously provided opportunities to try out my ideas on Ecuadorian audiences. Jay Sokolovsky introduced me to the Texcoco region for the first time and since then has continued to share his valuable insights. Frances Rothstein kindly took the time to read an early version of the manuscript and to provide comments and suggestions.

I am obliged to Pedro Pitarch for his exceptional writings on Tzeltal society, for his encouragement, and for giving me the opportunity to present my work in Trujillo. I have the greatest appreciation for Catharine Good's work on Nahuas in Guerrero, Mexico. Her collaboration and support have been invaluable, and she and her students at the Escuela Nacional de Antropología e Historia did me the honor of reading and commenting on an earlier version of the manuscript in one of their seminars. Roy Wagner's brilliant work was my guide and inspiration during this project. I consider myself fortunate to have enjoyed his company, teachings, and encouragement on a number of occasions over the years.

I would like to thank everyone at the University of Arizona Press who contributed to the book's publication, and I am especially grateful to Allyson Carter for her interest and belief in my work. Two anonymous reviewers' careful readings and thoughtful suggestions and Sally Bennett's skillful editing have significantly improved this final version.

Finally, the residents of Tepetlaoxtoc who shared their time and thoughts with me have been central to this project. They contributed to this book not just "data" but knowledge, understandings, and theories. In particular, I would like to recognize my debt to Crispín Soto Varela for sharing his wisdom and to his whole family for their warmth and hospitality.

THE VILLAGE IS LIKE A WHEEL

ONE

Introduction

Interdependence and the Production of Active Subjectivity

In this book, I propose an approach to the study of social life in rural highland Mexican communities that integrates local understandings into anthropological thinking. I have attempted to formulate this approach because I felt that my informants' understandings of their practices did not fit into standard anthropological formulations about highland Mexican communities. This approach has helped me to conceptualize and describe various aspects of social life in the village of Tepetlaoxtoc in the Texcoco region of the state of Mexico. And while Tepetlaoxtoc, like all other highland villages, has its sociocultural specificities due to its particular insertion in wider historical processes, I believe that what I learned from my informants there is relevant for some, if not all, of the communities throughout this world region. More specifically, I believe that it suggests how we[1] might rethink some of the classic anthropological topics in the region: cargo systems and community organization; family; and ethnicity/modernization. Furthermore, since this approach suggests the limitations of certain standard anthropological formulations, I also see it as part of a broader disciplinary effort, led mostly by authors working in other world regions such as Melanesia and Amazonia, to use our informants' understandings to help increase our awareness of the cultural particularity or ethnocentricity of our supposedly universal theoretical concepts.

When I began my research in Tepetlaoxtoc in 2001, I was struck by villagers' preoccupation with *los de afuera* (those from outside): recent migrants to the community who had moved there from Mexico City's working class neighborhoods in search of inexpensive housing. They listed "los de afuera" as one of the village's principal problems, and when I asked them to elaborate, they stated that those from outside have different customs (*costumbres*), such as stealing and using drugs. Getting villagers to talk about concrete examples of these thieves and drug addicts was difficult, but when discussing another favorite local topic of conversation—fiestas and other communal undertakings—they were more concrete about the defects of los de afuera. I frequently heard them complain that those from outside *"no quieren participar"* ("do not want to participate") or *"no quieren cooperar"* ("do not want to cooperate"), referring, I thought at the time, to the fact that los de afuera resist contributing time, effort, or money to the fiestas for patron saints and to community projects such as paving streets, the upkeep and extension of the water system, and the upkeep of the cemetery.

I assumed this to mean that the difference between those from outside and villagers is that the former spend their money on consumer items following individual or family interests and the latter spend theirs for the good of the community and in return receive a place in the community's social structure as well as prestige. This understanding fit quite well with standard anthropological descriptions of highland Mexican villages in which community boundaries are reinforced and its social structure is constituted through people's participation in the cargo system (see Cancian 1965; Wolf 1955). The cargo system refers to a series of unpaid posts or offices that community members occupy on a rotating basis to fulfill tasks of local government, community organization, and religious service. According to anthropologists, when community members participate in this system by holding cargos, they also occupy positions in the village social structure, often described as the civil-religious hierarchy. People who do not participate are thus excluded from this structure and stand outside of the community.

As my research progressed, however, I began to suspect that I had misunderstood their complaint about outsiders in a subtle but significant way. Villagers noted specific people who had been *mayordomos*—a mayordomo is the cargo holder who is in charge of putting on a fiesta for a patron saint—and had spent quite a lot of money but were nevertheless considered to have done a poor job and to be outsiders, or at least like outsiders, because they had not involved others. These villagers explained that taking on a *mayordomía* is difficult because it involves spending a lot of one's money but that the hardest part is the effort required to go around and collect *cooperaciones* (monetary contributions) from others. This involves not just knocking on doors and receiving monetary contributions but also the challenge of motivating potential donors to act, of convincing them, and transforming their reticent subjective state to one of enthusiasm, or *gusto*. The problem with outsiders, I began to see, was not their unwillingness to contribute time or money to the community but rather the fact that they thought they could do things, such as put on a fiesta, on their own. In contrast, I realized that villagers consistently put emphasis on the importance of doing things *entre todos* (among everyone) and on how people need each other. It also became apparent to me that people did not need each other simply for accomplishing larger projects such as putting on fiestas but for something more basic: for being able to act. What villagers meant when they described outsiders as "individualistic" was not precisely selfishness but rather the notion that their motivation to act could come from within and not from another person.

One informant used a clear image to explain to me how villagers understand the putting on of fiestas, although I believe that the same explanation could be used for other community projects. He said that the community is like a wheel, with villagers making up the wheel itself and the mayordomo's *compañeros* (companions or helpers) as the spokes, and the mayordomo's job is to start it rolling. He said that the villagers and their monetary contributions are set and ready to go, but they require the mayordomo to set them in motion. Thus, to return to the contrast between standard anthropological and local understandings, we could say that the mayordomo does not produce social relations, social structure, or the community as anthropologists, including myself, have usually thought—these things are already there and ready to go. Rather, he produces action in other people or, in local terms, *participación* (participation), as well as a subjective state of willingness, or "gusto." The sum of everyone's participation that the mayordomo produces is described as *"hacer la fiesta entre todos"* ("doing the fiesta among everyone"), which refers literally to the fact that everyone who participates and not just the mayordomo puts on the fiesta. This fiesta done among everyone is the rolling wheel.

In general, among residents of Tepetlaoxtoc, a considerable amount of human effort is directed to the objective of the production[2] of *active subjectivity in others* rather than to that of producing *things*, such as community, traditions, or material goods. It is not that they do not produce things or that these things do not matter, but that this production of things is usually a means for or a by-product of the production of active subjectivity. Villagers are concerned with producing active subjectivity in others because this is what they most highly value. What matters most about practices such as fiestas are the people involved, or, more accurately, their actions and subjective states. Villagers clearly express their appreciation of the beauty of the fiesta's decorations, fireworks, and music, but this beauty would be meaningless without people's participation. I use the term *active subjectivity* to denote the fact that what they produce is not simply action in others but also a subjective state of willingness to perform the action. It is important to add that this production does not refer to *controlling* other persons: the action produced belongs to the actor and not to the producer. The former needs someone else to cause him to act, but when he does so it is because he wants to. As I mention above, the sum of this production of active subjectivities in a given context is referred to as "doing something among everyone," which principally signals people's need for each other to get something done and even to be able to act. I refer here to this mutual need as *interdependence* to highlight that this mode of personhood or action cannot be categorized as either independent or dependent.

[handwritten marginalia: A.S. is endured but is a choice]

I am not the first to note the contrast between Mesoamerican notions of personhood and action and our own. Jorge Klor de Alva, for instance, referring to the colonial period, states that

> for unacculturated natives there was no autonomous will at the core of the self since every human being was a microcosm reflecting the forces that made up the cosmos at large. Furthermore, there was no clear boundary between personal will and the supernatural and natural forces that governed the universe. . . . Therefore, behavior, performance, and punctiliousness, rather than will, contemplation, or motivation were the key concerns of the Nahua who strove to be moral. . . . Consequently, the boundary between the individual self (the sole object of a Christian-type salvation), other selves, and what Westerners would consider nonanimate objects was completely permeable. (1997:183, 185)

Gary Gossen, meanwhile, posits that this lack of an individual continues into the present, noting that the Mesoamerican person is linked to supernatural forces, co-essences, or souls "that influence the destiny of the self. These forces lie outside the body and are thus not easy to change or manipulate" (1994:557). Further, "the factors that determine individual fate and fortune are always to be understood and reflected on as phenomena that are *predestined* but also, secondarily, *subject to the agency and will of others*, both human and supernatural" (1994:566; emphasis in original). Consequently, there is "a deep skepticism about individual autonomy and the very idea of a 'self-made' individual who is guided only by pragmatic self-interest. In short, these ideas seem to deny the very pillars of Western liberalism" (1994:567).

James Taggart, in his work on a Nahuat community in the northern sierra of the state of Puebla, describes a version of personhood in which "acting autonomously is inconsistent with the communal organization of work" (2007:6). People in conflict frequently accuse each other of "'acting big,' or *hueichihua*, a phrase that means to act egotistically rather than in accord with the demands of the group" (2007:54), while working together produces *tazohtliz* (love) (2007:87). Doren Slade, describing the Nahuat community of Chignautla in the same region, notes, "The conceptualization of social life captured in the term *makwis* [a form of interpersonal assistance] depicts a mode of interaction in which each partner is bound by the actions of the other" (1992:105). She contrasts this conceptualization of social life with Cancian's (1965) and other anthropologists' notion that people are motivated by self-enhancement and prestige: "Self-seeking motivations are experienced by Chignautecos as a distraction from appropriate intentions, and an individual who hopes to have an impact on the general population rather than quietly serve the saints would have to disregard what would commonly be expected to occur from coercing the saints" (1992:114). Note that acting upon or coercing an other, in this case the saint, is considered appropriate but self-enhancement is not.

In Nahua communities in the state of Guerrero, Catharine Good Eshelman finds a similar emphasis on the collective organization of work, or *tequitl*, a concept that goes beyond the capitalist idea of work to include "all use of physical, spiritual, intellectual, artistic or emotional human energy to accomplish a specific objective, defined in social terms" (2004a:137; my translation). People always work for the benefit of others (2004b:155), and when they do, they pass along their *chicahualiztli* or *fuerza* (force), which is a sort of vital energy that has a generative capacity that makes its recipient's work productive and visible (2004a:137). "A person that works, but does so alone, 'gets tired,' sweats but 'doesn't see their work'" (2004a:137–38). Only by exchanging tequitl and fuerza with others does work become productive.

In Tepetlaoxtoc, villagers' explanations of personhood and action could be considered perhaps more secular, without explicit references to something like fuerza or co-essences (although the saints are still important actors), but I think the resonance of these other descriptions with what I refer to as interdependence and the production of active subjectivities is apparent. I intend this book as a contribution to these efforts to understand and clarify highland Mexican notions of personhood and action. I also hope to demonstrate that once these local notions of personhood and action are incorporated into our thinking as anthropologists, some of the classic topics of Mesoamerican ethnography take on a very different appearance.

Cargos, fiestas, and other community endeavors constitute one of these classic topics that I attempt to reformulate in this book through the lens of interdependence and the production of active subjectivity. Another context in which others (Good Eshelman 2004b, 2005; López Millán 2008; Ramírez Sánchez 2003; Regehr 2005) and I have observed such principles at work is that of interfamilial and intrafamilial relations. At the interfamilial level, people produce active subjectivity in others when they want to put on a life-cycle fiesta, such as a baptism or a wedding, and they provoke others to participate by providing what is referred to as *ayuda* (help) in the form of labor or material objects. These exchanges before the actual celebration are considered part of the fiesta, perhaps the most important part. The success of a life-cycle fiesta is not measured by the attendance at the celebration itself but rather by the people who provided ayuda and thus "accompanied" the family putting on the fiesta (López Millán 2008).

At the intrafamilial level, *estar juntos* (to be together) is constituted by exchanges between parents and their sons and daughters (Ramírez Sánchez 2003; Regehr 2005). Parents care for their young children, which in turn causes the latter to act as sons and daughters and to provide ayuda to their parents. Sons and daughters provide this ayuda by doing chores around the house starting when they are physically capable, by working alongside their parents in the fields, in workshops, or on construction sites and by giving all or part of their salaries to their parents. Even sons and daughters living as far away as the United States who send back their earnings as ayuda are considered to be "together" with their parents. Sons and daughters continue providing this ayuda until they marry, which has the cumulative effect of causing their parents to act as such and to provide them with ayuda in the form of paying for their wedding and giving them a plot of land on which to build a house. Parents and sons and daughters need and value each other not only in a material sense—this is more than just a collective effort at survival—but also because they cause each other to act or more specifically to act as parents and sons and daughters. These exchanges of ayuda between generations constitute the motor of the life cycle or of social reproduction (Magazine and Ramírez Sánchez 2007). Such actions are what people most value; it could even be said that they constitute persons and social life.

A third context in which I explore the importance of the production of active subjectivity is what we usually refer to as interethnic relations or, more specifically for the Mexican case, the relationship between the so-called urban, modern, mestizo world and the so-called rural, traditional, indigenous one. This is also commonly referred to as modernization or as resistance to modernization. We usually see ethnic groups as categories of people distinguished by their production of different kinds of *things*, also referred to as their culture. In Tepetlaoxtoc, however, an "other" is recognized not by the things he has produced and possesses but through a direct interaction that produces action and subjectivity. Another way to put this would be to say that villagers recognize an other through a relation of interdependence or interconnectedness and not at an objective distance. Thus, residents are less interested in a comparison of different cultures than in the efficacy of other persons, including neighbors or outsiders, in the interdependent production of action and subjectivity. Outsiders with urban origins rarely fare well in such evaluations of efficacy because they do not share villagers' understanding of otherness and of production.

Villagers tend to evaluate the objects of modernity such as technology along the same lines. Rather than the choice between modernizing and leaving behind their culture versus resisting modernization and preserving it, they are concerned with the effects that things such as technology will have on interdependence and the production of active subjectivity. Roads, for example (see Kuromiya 2006, 2010), are useful if they facilitate transportation to the city, where people can earn money that they will then use as cooperaciones and ayuda. However, roads can also be negatively viewed if they facilitate the incursion into the village of urbanites with their businesses and other practices that can have an individualizing effect in the sense that they make people think they can act on their own. I believe that this local approach to what we usually think of as modernity or urban culture helps explain why a village such as Tepetlaoxtoc can appear to be modern and fully integrated into the global capitalist economy at the same time that its residents clearly distinguish between themselves and "city people." In other words, instead of representing a case of modernization in the sense of modernity displacing a local culture, I believe that the change that we are observing is more like a local reaction to and an appropriation of aspects of modernity and capitalism.

A proposal for rethinking each of these three topics—(1) the fiestas celebrated for patron saints and the so-called cargo system, or civil-religious hierarchy; (2) family or kinship; and (3) the ethnic relationship between indigenous people and modern, urban, or mestizo people—is put forward in subsequent chapters. I should note that my decision to divide my discussion and my ethnography into these three classic and heavily studied topics in the anthropology of Mexico emerges from my own experience as an anthropologist and my objective to reach an anthropological audience. I am not proposing that the region's residents would divide up their lives in this manner, and how or if they would do so at all is the topic for another book.

Because my overall objective is not to describe social life in Tepetlaoxtoc but to propose an approach to studying aspects of social life in highland Mexican communities in general, I employ a method that involves setting up a contrast between this approach based on local understandings and standard modern Western conceptualizations, usually produced by anthropologists. I employ this contrast because I wish to convey that this approach is not simply another to be applied alongside of certain traditional theories; rather, it is intended to suggest a direction for replacing those traditional theories along with the ethnocentric assumptions on which they are based. For example, when I state that the mayordomo's role is to produce action and subjective states in others, I do not mean to suggest this as a new route to reproducing social structure and community boundaries. Instead, I am proposing that while *we* may be concerned with the reproduction of social structure and community boundaries, *our informants* are really concerned with the production of action and subjectivity. In other words, I wish to make explicit that it is we who assume that human life consists of individuals, naturally endowed with the ability to act, producing, knowing, and living in a world of objects, including what anthropologists usually recognize as culture, community, social structure, and social relations. These assumptions are, of course, difficult for us to recognize as such since they appear to us as natural and universal. However, if we can manage to leave behind these assumptions for at least a moment and to see that, possibly, our informants do not share them, I believe that the contrast provided by novel interpretations of our ethnographic data can help us to become aware of ethnocentrisms in our conceptual tools and to begin to make changes in our approach.

Even though this method helps me to communicate my proposal, it obviously has its limitations as well. Principally, it falsely posits homogeneous highland Mexican and modern-Western conceptualizations of social life. I am undoubtedly forcing complex, heterogeneous, and constantly changing practices into two static categories, thereby sacrificing descriptive accuracy to try to make a more general point. In other words, I emphasize and may even exaggerate the importance of the production of active subjectivity and of interdependence to make my point, even though, in the process, I may downplay or even neglect other aspects of my informants' lives.

Another potential problem with this kind of contrast is that it can imply that highland Mexicans live in a separate world from the modern West. However, I believe that Tepetlaoxtoc's proximity to Mexico City and its integration into global capitalism and national politics help to lead me away from such a portrayal, at least in certain parts of the text. Rather than portraying two separate worlds, I try to describe different manners of understanding and acting upon the same world. Further, I attempt to show that these two manners are hardly independent of each other. Tepetlaoxtoc's residents often conceptualize their lives in contrast to life in the city. In fact, the contrast that I propose here is in large part derived from a contrast that my informants themselves make. They helped me to see more clearly the manners in which city people's ideas, and, in particular, their individualism and obsession with things, were not applicable to village life. In my exaggeration of the significance of the production of active objectivity and of interdependence, I am thus echoing my informants and their constant effort to keep at bay those aspects of "city ways" that they view negatively but must face and even adopt on a daily basis. It could be said that it is also necessary to exaggerate such claims in my writing to counter the dominant modes of modern Western thought that surround and permeate us not just in our work but, at times, in our everyday lives as well.

Considering the fact that villagers are constantly confronting and even living these city ways, I must admit that once again my division between "villagers" and "city people" represents something of a distortion. For the purpose of argument, I write as if the division were well-defined and clear, but this is not always the case. Often, for example, villagers can act indistinguishably from city people, and vice versa, since many "city people" are from rural areas. Villagers, in fact, demonstrate at least two different manners of acting like city people. At times, they can appear to be concerned with the production of things when they are really still concerned with the production of active subjectivity. In other words, they take on city ways for their own purposes (a process described in chapter 5). However, at other moments, they may truly dedicate themselves to the production of things, a stance that can be highly effective in business and politics but is quickly criticized as being *individualista* (individualistic) or *presumido* (arrogant). The relationship of "city people" (and here I include myself and many other anthropologists) to the production of things and, perhaps, to something like the production of persons is, I suspect, equally complex. The fact that I was able to grasp this alternative to the production of things, and hopefully my readers will be able to as well, suggests that we are not limited to our "modern Western ways." But if this is a study of "us," it is only a study of us as anthropologists and not of us in a more general sense—that kind of study would require its own fieldwork.

Beyond the Production of Culture and Society

Many of the anthropological studies of highland Mexican and Guatemalan communities published before the mid-1990s could be placed in one of two categories: those concerned with social structure, often combined with political economy (e.g., Aguirre Beltrán 1973; Cancian 1965, 1992; Carrasco 1961; Chance and Taylor 1985; Greenberg 1981; Nash 1958; Nutini 1968; Nutini, Carrasco, and Taggart 1976; Taggart 1991 [1975]; Vogt 1969; Wolf 1955) and those focused on belief systems or worldview (e.g., Bricker 1973; Broda and Báez-Jorge 2001; Gossen 1974; Guiteras-Holmes 1961; Hunt 1977; López Austin 1980; Vogt 1976). These focuses were different but not opposed to each other, and some authors produced works in both categories (e.g., Vogt 1969 and 1976) or linked the two together in the same study (e.g., Taggart 1997 [1983]). I suggest that these two groups of studies shared a common characteristic: they both treated their findings as an object of study to be described and analyzed, often in innovative and sophisticated manners, but maintaining those findings on a separate epistemological level from their analytical approaches. In other words, they did not see the local ideas and understandings they were studying as something that could enter into dialogue with or contribute to anthropological theory. Highland Mesoamerican belief systems or worldviews were something to be recorded and analyzed but not to be learned from in a practical sense or taken seriously as a contrasting theory of human life.

More recently, numerous authors have attempted to incorporate local concepts and understandings into their analysis (e.g., Good Eshelman 2004a, 2004b, 2005; Gossen 1994; Klor de Alva 1997; Monaghan 1990, 1995, 2008; Neurath 2008; Pitarch 2003a, 2003b; Slade 1992; Taggart 2007). These authors have taken important steps toward contrasting local thinking with our own and toward understanding how our informants build their worlds on their own terms. This kind of approach is, however, recent in the case of highland Mexico, and much remains to be done in this direction. The ideas of three anthropologists who work outside the region—Roy Wagner, Marilyn Strathern, and Eduardo Viveiros de Castro—provide valuable models for how to use ethnographic data and local understandings to increase awareness of the cultural particularity of our theoretical tools and thus their limitations for understanding other people's lives. The anthropology of Mesoamerica would greatly benefit from the kind of critical revision of anthropological problems that these authors have brought about for Melanesia and Amazonia.

Building on David Schneider's (1980 [1968]) conclusion that the notion of kinship as buffer between nature and culture is particular to modern Western society, Roy Wagner (1981 [1975]) examines the implications of anthropology's use of the concept of culture to study peoples who do not see themselves as inventing a culture in which to live. Wagner's argument—which I should admit has been here translated largely into my own terms and edited to highlight my own interests—begins with the proposal that human beings create the worlds in which they live, but we must define a segment of this creation as something that has not been created at all, as something innate. In other words, we must blind ourselves to a segment of our creation. We require this illusion of fixity to give form and meaning to the other segment of our creation that we define as the appropriate arena for human action. In reality we are constantly creating what we see as innate, but for our inventions and innovations to appear as such we oppose them to a supposedly fixed starting point. According to Wagner, in modern society, we have created nature as our fixed starting point. In persons, nature takes the form of our particularity or our individuality. Human action, meanwhile, involves building upon nature: what we usually refer to as culture. And because our particularity and individuality are innate, what we build should be directed toward the general, the conventional, or the collective, or what we could call the social. In contrast, among "traditional" peoples, the segments are reversed and the innate is imagined to be the conventional or collective aspect of things that we usually think of as culture. Human action, meanwhile, is supposed to be directed toward particularization, differentiation, or individualization.

At least for me, this second manner of defining the innate and appropriate arena for action is more difficult to imagine, but I think it becomes clearer through examples presented below from the work of Strathern and Viveiros de Castro and then later in my own ethnography. This difficulty makes our task as anthropologists challenging, to say the least. However, as Wagner argues, the matter is more complicated when we do our work without taking into account the particularity of our own version of what is innate and what is created. Because we go everywhere expecting to find *their* version of *culture*, we of course end up finding it: in the form of kinship systems, social structure, technologies, myths, and rituals. The problem is not that these things do not exist at all, but rather that we misunderstand the place they occupy in people's lives. We report them as what life for such-and-such group is all about, when in reality, for them we have just described the starting point, basically ignoring what they see as their action, creativity, and productivity. One of my main objectives in this book is to suggest that our focuses in Mexico and Mesoamerica on civil-religious hierarchy and community, peasant families, kinship units, and indigenous culture are examples of this kind of misunderstanding.

As with Wagner, my description of Strathern's (1988) critique reduces it to the part that interests me here, omitting many of the directions in which she develops her arguments. Building on Wagner's focus on the nature/culture dichotomy, Strathern examines anthropology's unquestioned employment of the individual/society dichotomy. She notes that much of our work is based on the unspoken assumption that individual persons are capable of acting on their own and that this action is generally directed toward uniting individuals in relationships and society. She links this assumption to the fact that we live in a world of commodities and the figure of the commodity is extended to our actions, so that persons are expected to own, control, and be responsible for their own actions. She contrasts these assumptions about agency and action with Melanesian understandings in which the basic goal or problem for people is not creating the social, but rather creating persons capable of action. In Melanesia, persons are social from even before birth—they are constituted by all of the social relations that define who they are. In this generalized social state, they lack the specificity required to carry out a certain action. Before acting, they must be particularized; a specific aspect of their person must be drawn out. This drawing out is accomplished by the process we usually call exchange. A donor detaches a part of himself and gives it (himself) to the recipient, thereby causing a shift in the latter, drawing out this specificity and the possibility for action. For Strathern, one of the important implications of this kind of action is that actors do not cause their own actions. Agency and action are split. This does not mean, however, that the agent controls or dominates the actor. The relationship between actor and action, just like that between donor and gift, is not one of alienable property, and although the agency can be separated from the actor, his action cannot, even if he did not cause it. Another implication of this manner of acting that is significant to me here is that there is a quite literal connectedness between persons and things and between persons. In other words, sociality is not just about separate persons or things coming together in the sense of aligning their objectives. Rather, it involves the elimination of boundaries between persons and things or between persons whose objectives may remain separate.

Strathern's conceptualization of agency and action in Melanesia has been of great help to me in my efforts to imagine these same things in my own research. People in the Texcoco region insist in many contexts on the importance of "doing things among everyone" or "doing things together," which we could easily interpret to mean that individual people must be brought together to align their objectives and act collectively as a family, community, and so forth. However, I believe that such an interpretation makes the kind of mistake that Strathern attempts to bring to our awareness: imposing our idea that "togetherness," in the sense of creating collectivity, is a problem when the real problem is the "doing." In other words, the problem is not acting to produce sociality, as has generally been assumed in the anthropology of indigenous Mexico, but rather getting others, to whom one is already related socially, to act. And again in a manner comparable to what Strathern describes, people in Tepetlaoxtoc get others to act by giving a part of themselves to the other person, thereby creating a literal "togetherness" that may include, but is not based on, sharing objectives or acting collectively.

Eduardo Viveiros de Castro's work (1998, 2004), based on his research in Amazonia, provides additional language and concepts for achieving the shift in focus that is my objective here. He claims that while we imagine a world in which there is one nature and multiple cultures, Amerindians imagine a world in which there is one culture and multiple natures. This "multinaturalism" refers to the fact that they consider animals to be persons but in a different form or with a different body. Although these persons have different bodies, they all share the same culture with humans; that is, they live in the same kinds of communities, have the same kinds of kin relations and marriage proscriptions, and so forth. Humans and animals "apprehend reality from distinct points of view" (2004:466), which is why we cannot see each others' personness and culture. Animals, however, see themselves as humans, inhabiting villages and houses, and they see humans as animals, either as game or as prey (2004:466). In this multi-natural world, even inanimate objects lack a fixed form as, for example, "jaguars see blood as manioc beer, [and] vultures see the maggots in rotting meat as grilled fish" (2004:466). Thus, "the notion of matter as a universal substrate seems wholly absent from Amazonian ontologies. Reflexive self-hood, not material objectivity, is the potential common ground of being" (2004:466–67).

At this point, we get to the part of Viveiros de Castro's formulation that most interests me: For us, because we do believe in this universal substrate of matter, "[t]o know, then, is to *desubjectify*" (2004:468; emphasis in original) or to objectify, stripping away subjectivity to get the "real" object world. "Objectification is the name of our game; what is not objectified remains unreal and abstract. The form of the other is *the thing*" (2004:468; emphasis in original). I would add that life for us is not just about knowing objects but about objectification of all sorts. Returning to Wagner's language for a moment, we see the appropriate arena for human action as consisting of acting upon objects and transforming them to produce new ones. And to return to Strathern's argument, to act upon another person is considered inappropriate; it is treating them as an object. The other, for us, since we are subjects, is *distinct*. In contrast, "Amerindian shamanism is guided by the opposite ideal. To know is to personify, to take on the point of view of that which must be known. Shamanic knowledge aims at something that is a someone—another subject. The form of the other is *the person*" (2004:468; emphasis in original). The other for them is the *same*. Again, I would add an important point. At least among people in the Texcoco region, subjectification or personification is not just about knowing: it is the appropriate arena for human action in general. As we will see, action is all about producing active subjectivity in others, and objects are simply a means to this end or influence the form this production takes. Another way to put all of this would be to say that *we* live together as subjects in a world of objects, while *they* live in a world of persons, mediated by objects.

Thus, while the Texcoco region lacks the spectacular human animals and shamanic bodily transformations that Viveiros de Castro describes, his concepts prove quite useful in my efforts to talk about distinct kinds of human action or production: our production of objects versus their production of active subjects. His formulation on otherness also aids in my exploration, undertaken in chapter 5, of how my informants deal with what we usually think of as ethnic difference. While we create a distinctive culture for our others to be able to recognize and interact with them as such, my informants approach people from the city with interest in the latter's subjectivity—their sameness—and are often disappointed, because urbanites live their subjectivity in a manner so different that it is unrecognizable to people from the region as such. In reaction, villagers categorize city people as if they were objects: as insignificant or foolish. To put this differently, with their apparent lack of subjectivity, city people are not significant enough to qualify as an other.

I would like to add some general comments on my use of these authors' works and the critical perspective they propose, with an eye to anticipating some frustrations, doubts, and criticisms. First, I would like to note something about the difficulty with working with Wagner's, Strathern's, and Viveiros de Castro's critiques. I would say that they are exciting, at least for those of us drawn to the discipline by its interest in cultural diversity and the destabilizing of our basic assumptions, but at the same time they are hard to grasp and even harder to maintain a grasp upon. At least in my own thinking, they seem to constantly slip away, probably because in my everyday life I need the illusions of fixity and purposefulness afforded by the nature/culture dichotomy. Because of this difficulty of going against our everyday thinking, I believe that what we often do is to ignore them or to heed them only superficially, dropping certain terms from our anthropological vocabulary, such as *culture*, but without changing our concepts and our overall approach.

Another problem with these critiques, with their us/them dichotomies and their descriptions of ways of living life very different from our own, is that they make us uncomfortable in the wake of postcolonial or Orientalist critiques of the discipline. I think, however, that an abandonment of our efforts to understand difference would be a case of throwing out the baby with the bathwater. Orientalist critiques were aimed at the manner in which anthropologists, among others, imposed their own culturally particular version of otherness, which, as these critiques revealed, has more to do with defining the "modern West" than with understanding other ways of living life. I do not think that the point of these critiques was to deny difference or the importance of trying to understand it. Rather, it seems to me that the kind of critique described above is precisely what we need because it questions old ways of understanding otherness and tries out new ways based on a combination of greater conceptual self-awareness and ethnographic data. This is not to say that these new understandings are the final word, and they are by no means free from problems of ethnocentrism and Orientalism, which is precisely why the effort must be ongoing. The alternative seems to be a denial that difference exists or, perhaps, ever existed (see Viveiros de Castro 2004:483n36). And even worse, this denial usually takes on the form of Occidentalism, reducing everyone's lives to how we see ourselves. So while we can definitely find evidence of "globalization," I suspect that our recent avoidance of difference has as much to do with fear of "Orientalizing" or "exoticizing" as it does with the hard facts of globalization.

This denial of difference is particularly acute in the anthropology of highland Mexico—perhaps because of its long history of colonization and Western influence—as is evidenced by the recent turn from studies of culture to studies of cultural and identity politics. I believe, however, that this makes our efforts to move beyond this denial and pay attention to local understandings of difference in the highland Mexican case all the more important if we wish to move beyond the spatial-temporal discourse that divides the world into traditional and modern. Studies that demonstrate drastic ontological differences between the modern Western world and the isolated communities of Melanesia and Amazonia do little to disturb this discourse. In fact, they could be said to help reproduce it. Studies in highland Mexico, in contrast, have the potential to upset this discourse precisely because they offer the opportunity to observe people doing something quite different in the very familiar world of the Spanish language, wage work, and globalized consumption.

Available Ethnic Categories: A Dilemma

While I am on the topic of ethnicity I should explain why I have avoided categorizing Tepetlaoxtoc's residents as indigenous, even while I set up an opposition between their understandings of social life and those understandings that I refer to as modern, urban, or even anthropological. In brief, I avoid this categorization because I do not want my readers to be distracted from my argument about the significance of local understandings by the question of whether or not Tepetlaoxtoc is indigenous. The threat of distraction is a significant one since such a question could be debated endlessly, and it is not clear to me that there is any benefit to be had from such a debate. The labeling of any highland community, even the most isolated, non-Spanish-speaking one, as indigenous is subject to suspicion because finding, five hundred years after the conquest, a pure prehispanic culture untainted by European influence is impossible. At the other extreme, it seems equally ridiculous to suggest that today's highland communities have nothing to do with the prehispanic past. Languages constitute a clear example, although not the only one. Even if "indigenous" languages have changed over the past five hundred years, incorporating Spanish words and structures, for example, they are still spoken. And even though Tepetlaoxtoc's residents no longer speak an indigenous language, I believe that some of the Spanish terms they use, such as *ayuda* (see chapter 4), are poor translations of Nahuatl words that continue to refer to highland Mexican concepts. James Maffie's (2003) description of prehispanic Nahua philosophy clearly resonates with their manner of approaching knowledge (see chapter 5). This continuity is not surprising, because the historical record now suggests that both Spanish and national rule had to accommodate to various aspects of community life (see Klor de Alva 1997; Lockhart 1994).

As I suggest in the previous section, this insistence on defining highland peoples in terms of their relation or lack thereof to a prehispanic past is part of a nation-building project that requires a distinctive indigenous past as well as evidence of progress in the form of the acculturation or modernization of formerly indigenous persons. To label certain people indigenous is to force them to represent in the present "that impossible thing of national desire" (Povinelli 2002:69): an utterly non-European past. Others, considered acculturated or "mestizo," are placed in the no-less-impossible position of having to represent the nation's successful process of modernization. Arbitrary definitions of indigenousness through specific traits such as language serve this nation-building project by ostensibly providing both indigenous and mestizo populations. Because of the benefits that the state or society in general offer to the representatives of these categories, self-definition is also drawn into this nation-building project. For example, we can easily understand if residents of many highland communities, including Tepetlaoxtoc, do not categorize themselves as indigenous, when we consider the social, economic, and political benefits of avoiding the stigma of backwardness associated with indigenousness. At the same time, it is understandable that other highland residents attempt to reap the benefits of categorizing themselves as indigenous offered by government agencies and through tourism. Of course, this kind of political-temporal discourse that denies contemporaneity or "co-evalness" in its ethnic categorizations is present in anthropological representations (Fabian 1983) as well as nation-building projects. Or, to capture the complexity of anthropological debates, it would be more accurate to state that we have participated both in finding these indigenous or acculturated things of national and anthropological desire and in demonstrating their impossibility. Judith Friedlander (1975), for example, exposes inauthentic indigenousness to uncover "real" acculturation, while Guillermo Bonfil Batalla (1973) exposes inauthentic acculturation to uncover "real" indigenousness.

My intention here is not to propose a revision of ethnic categories for contemporary Mexico (but see Bonfil Batalla 1973; Friedlander 1975; Robichaux and Magazine 2007), even if I do believe that such a revision is necessary. Rather, I hope to convince my readers not to let such preoccupations with authenticity and representation sidetrack them from what I *am* trying to do. To borrow some wording from Viveiros de Castro (2004): my argument here is about ontology, but I fear that our disciplinary "epistemological angst" will distract from it. I should also clarify that my avoidance of the label *indigenous* is not a denial of the importance of ethnic difference for understanding contemporary Mexican society. My argument here regarding a contrast between local understandings of social life versus standard modern, urban, or anthropological understandings obviously derives from this difference. Tepetlaoxtoc's residents themselves insist on the distinction between themselves and "city people" even though they do not phrase this distinction in terms of indigenousness and modernization. I realize, however, that my simple avoidance of certain labels such as *indigenous* and my replacement of them with others such as *local* and *rural highland Mexico* is not sufficient to eliminate the political-temporal discourse within which such labels function. As Johannes Fabian (1983) has argued, eliminating terms from our anthropological vocabulary does not necessarily have an effect on underlying discourse and categories. Because a simple change of terms will not do the trick, one of the discipline's main objectives should be to critique this political-temporal discourse and to help provide alternative approaches to otherness in order to move beyond it (Fabian 1983; Trouillot 1991). In other words, we need new ways of imagining difference and connectedness at the same time. My hope here is that my discussion in chapter 5 of the manner in which my informants deal with otherness makes at least a small contribution to this effort by providing us not just with new labels but with a conceptual alternative to approaching ethnicity.

Methodology

Most of the research on which this book is based was conducted in the village of Tepetlaoxtoc, about an hour's drive outside of Mexico City, during summers from 2001 to 2007. I did additional fieldwork on occasional visits during other times of the year, between 2001 and 2009. The summer fieldwork was conducted at the same time that I was supervising groups of graduate students participating in a *práctica de campo*—a sort of field school. In fact, the field school was what first drew me to the village and region, and I decided to take advantage of my stay by conducting my own research. Every year, during the first week of the field school, while staying at the Universidad Iberoamericana's fieldwork station in the village of Tepetlaoxtoc, the students and I would visit different villages in the region, speaking to residents and looking for housing for the students for the last five weeks of the program. During these last five weeks, the students would conduct fieldwork research in different villages, with many of them returning in the following years to do research for their master's thesis or Ph.D. dissertation. The visits to different villages as well as the students' research afforded me the opportunity to get to know the region as a whole and, since I was able to infect some of the students with my interests, to have my own thinking benefit from the results of their original research and creative analyses (e.g., Encarnación Ruiz 2004; Kuromiya 2006; Lechuga Paredes 2004; López Millán 2008; Velásquez Velásquez 2007). As the following chapters reveal, I continue to draw heavily on their work. I also draw heavily on a pair of theses based on two master's students' research in the neighboring state of Tlaxcala (Ramírez Sánchez 2003; Regehr 2005), where I conducted six weeks of ethnographic research in 2000, while learning how to run the field school from my colleague David Robichaux. The reader will also note that I have benefited substantially from the work of other researchers working in highland Mesoamerica. Their insights have led me to better understand my findings, and their data have helped me to see the broader regional significance of my analysis. I refer to these comparisons in many places throughout the text.

My research in Tepetlaoxtoc consisted primarily of informal interviews with villagers during my visits to their homes. At the beginning, unsure of what direction my research would take, I spoke to villagers about a variety of topics including cargos, fiestas, family organization, and economic activities, while I tried to pay attention to what topics the residents themselves were most interested in. It seemed to me at first that they were quite concerned with the effects of urban expansion upon their village. More specifically, they complained about the people from the city who had recently moved there in search of inexpensive housing, claiming that they were individualistic and even drug addicts and criminals. I started thinking that my focus would be their response to urban expansion. After a while, however, I began to understand that the villagers did not take the threat of city people or the problem of urban expansion so seriously. Instead, they seemed to like to talk about city people as a way of setting up a contrast with themselves: they were really talking to me about, or teaching me about, themselves and what life was all about for them. At this point, I really started "seeing" and paying attention to the themes that would become the main topics of this book: what I refer to as the production of active subjects, togetherness conceived of as prestations of inalienable parts of persons, and transformation or appropriation at the level of the person (instead of the level of culture or society).

I also attended as many community and barrio (neighborhood) fiestas as I could, usually as an invitee and sometimes as an informal mayordomo's aid, helping to serve food or decorate a church. I also occasionally participated in the fiestas through monetary contributions referred to locally as *cooperaciones*, collected by the mayordomo and his assistants. In part, I participated in this manner on behalf of the Universidad Iberoamericana and the fieldwork station: as he handed me my receipt, the mayordomo would usually explain that if the station required any sort of service from the municipal government it could be obtained by showing the receipts. But I had other motives as well. First, giving a *cooperación* provided an opportunity to participate in and observe firsthand this key moment in the production of subjects during the fiestas (see chapter 3). Second, this kind of participation always meant an invitation to the more private part of the fiesta: the meals provided by the mayordomo and his assistants. And third, a cooperación made it hard for the recipient to refuse my request for an interview at a later date.

I imagine that my frequent movement, throughout the text, among different geographic scales—Tepetlaoxtoc, the Texcoco region, and Mesoamerica—requires some explanation. First, the jump from Tepetlaoxtoc to Texcoco is not meant to imply homogeneity at the regional level. I would not even want to make such a claim at the village level. Variations of different sorts undoubtedly exist at the village and regional levels, and this is an important topic, perhaps even for fully understanding my own data, but because no study focused on this variation currently exists, its consideration will have to wait. When I make reference to the region level, this is usually a shorthand manner of saying that a student's findings in another village fit into the more general pattern of practices and understandings that I am describing for Tepetlaoxtoc. I realize that this similarity between two villages is not really sufficient evidence for making claims to the existence of region-wide practices and ways of understanding life, but I do not really have much interest in such claims here. My objective is not to prove homogeneity but rather to conceptualize certain approaches to life and to do so aided by research conducted by other people in other nearby sites.

The jumps between the village or region and Mesoamerica or indigenous Mexico are usually meant to be suggestive. I have found numerous similarities between my findings and those of colleagues who have worked in other parts of Mesoamerica. These similarities have led me to suspect and to propose that what I argue here has relevance for the rest of, or at least other parts of, this world region. It is important to clarify that this relevance is at the level of approach and analysis and not at the level of an empirical reality. I have no intention of denying Mesoamerica's heterogeneity or to make claims about region-wide sociocultural patterns. Rather, my objective is to suggest that the shift in analysis that I propose here may be relevant to other researchers and their research sites. In other words, I am interested in making a contribution to the anthropological study in Mesoamerica, not to statements or records of its empirical reality. This proposal is hardly definitive, and my hope is that my colleagues will build on and even redirect my efforts, but I would be disappointed, I must admit, if this book were read as just a study of Tepetlaoxtoc or of Texcoco.

In the following chapter, I provide a brief description of Tepetlaoxtoc and of the Texcoco region. Including such a chapter may seem to contradict my statement above regarding the book not being about the village or region.

My reason for including it is that despite my theoretical aspirations, my style of exposition remains within the anthropological tradition of working from the specific to the general. In other words, I construct my analytical proposal through the presentation of ethnography, and I follow the traditional disciplinary belief that a description of the local context provides a concrete setting that in turn enables the reader to more easily imagine the people and the lives about which he is reading. In each of the next three chapters, I propose how attention to the production of active subjectivity and to interdependence can help us to rethink a different classic topic in Mesoamerican anthropology.

Chapter 3 begins with an outline of the history of anthropological interest in cargo systems and then suggests that the assumption that they were primarily about social structure seems to have distracted from action-oriented local interests in the same practices. I then go on to describe these action-oriented interests in Tepetlaoxtoc, starting with the local precept that the fiesta should be put on *entre todos* (by everyone), which implies that the mayordomo's main task is not to sponsor the fiesta himself but rather to provoke others' participation. Villagers criticize people who try to put on fiestas on their own for being arrogant or individualistic. Subsequently, I describe in further detail what is implied by the fact that villagers must be caused to act by others. I discuss what it means for them "to participate" in fiestas through monetary donations, how it can be that these actions are considered both obligatory and voluntary, and why villagers insist that they may achieve recognition but do not gain prestige through cargo service.

In chapter 4, I begin by positing a contrast between the common anthropological assumption that family in highland Mexican communities is about producing and distributing the material things necessary for survival and reproduction and my own proposal that in the Texcoco region this distribution of things is also a means to the end of producing action in others and creating a literal togetherness through the exchange of inalienable objects. I then illustrate the workings of these exchanges of what is referred to locally as *ayuda* (help) at the inter- and intrafamily levels. At the interfamily level, several parallels with village-wide fiestas described in the previous chapter are revealed. For example, what matters most about celebrations of life-cycle rituals are not the fiestas themselves but rather the invitations that one family extends to others to provide ayuda and then the actual provision involved in the preparation for the fiesta. At the intrafamily level, I demonstrate how being a father, mother, daughter, or son consists of working to provide ayuda to the opposing generation. Further, the interdependence between generations is evidenced by the fact that these donations provoke a complementary reaction in the recipient, so that children cause their parents to bring them up and parents cause their children to take care of them in their old age.

Chapter 5 opens with a discussion of the manner in which anthropologists have generally treated the relationship of Mexico's indigenous, rural population to the modern, urban world. We have usually conceptualized this relationship as one between two opposing cultures, and our principal concern has been with how a process of modernization occurs or why it does not. In contrast, I show how Tepetlaoxtoc's residents see and know the urban "other" for its actions and subjectivity and not for its things, such as its culture. I then explain how this manner of perceiving the other leads to negative views of "city people," who usually fail to interact in the interdependent manner that villagers expect. Next, I use ethnographic examples to demonstrate that when villagers, individually or collectively, take an interest in aspects of modern-urban culture, they do so on their own terms, incorporating these things into their lives with the goal of achieving a situationally defined form of well-being rather than a universal version of progress. I then discuss the fact that this incorporation is achieved at the level of the person—rather than that of culture or society—through a process of practical, as opposed to theoretical, learning. They are thus able to appropriate aspects of the modern-urban world in a form that they value: not as things but as ways of acting and being a subject directed toward interdependence. To close this chapter, so as not to give the impression that Texcoco's residents are exempt from global capitalism's and the national state's domination and influence, I place their approach to modernity in the historically and geographically specific political-economic context that has allowed it to flourish.

TWO

The Texcoco Region and the Village of Tepetlaoxtoc

The Texcoco region occupies the northeast corner of the Valley of Mexico, separated from Mexico City's urban sprawl by the nearly unpopulated, 16-kilometer-wide, dry Texcoco Lake bed. The city of Texcoco, with its population of about 120,000, is located on the eastern shore of the lakebed, with the region extending out from the city to the south, east, and north. Heading east, there is a gradual and then a steeper rise up to the Sierra of Tlaloc, which divides the Valley of Mexico from the neighboring state of Tlaxcala. Anthropologists working in the region have typically followed Ángel Palerm and Eric Wolf (1972) in dividing it into four topographical subregions: (1) the plain, at 2,250 meters above sea level, where we find the city of Texcoco and a series of villages running north and south along the shore of the lakebed; (2) the foothills with another string of villages (including Tepetlaoxtoc) at an altitude of approximately 2,400 meters above sea level; (3) the "eroded belt," a subregion that was densely inhabited in prehispanic times but was subsequently abandoned due to erosion; and (4) the sierra, with still another string of villages at an altitude of about 2,750 meters. Of course, the geographic reality is somewhat more complex, because the villages are not so neatly aligned in strings and more than a few are difficult to classify.

When Palerm and Wolf (1972) described the region in terms of these four topographical subregions they were really interested in conceptualizing not its divisions but rather its integration by means of an irrigation system. According to these authors, the prehispanic Texcocan state constituted an example of a process of urban development in which the state preceded rather than grew out of the construction of an irrigation system (1972). However, their findings did suggest that the irrigation system, mostly constructed under the rule of Netzahualcoyotl in the fifteenth century, resulted in a greater integration of the different settlements in the area (1972). The system channeled water from springs in the sierra to the villages lower down for agricultural purposes. This integration allowed the Texcocan state to occupy an important position in preconquest politics in central highland Mexico, forming part of the "Triple Alliance" together with Tenochtitlan and Tlacopan. After the conquest, with the dismantling of the state and a switch from intensive agriculture to wool production under Spanish rule, the region took on a marginal position in relation to the Spanish capital in Tenochtitlan/Mexico City (1972). The irrigation system continued to operate, as it still does today, in a decentralized and incomplete manner with the "center" of the system now in the villages in the sierra where the springs are located. The residents there control the flow of water, letting enough pass for irrigation in some of the foothill villages, but the lower half of the system, reaching down to the plains villages, is no longer in operation.

While Palerm's interest in the region was principally historical, he also took advantage of its proximity to Mexico City to train students to conduct ethnographic research. Many of these students adopted this four-part topographical division and applied it to contemporary life in the region. This application is most clearly seen in Marisol Pérez Lizaur's (1977) region-wide study that compares social and demographic aspects of villages from the different subregions. She found that in the different subregions, the villages are in different moments or stages of a process consisting of an increase in population density and of an accompanying shift from extensive to intensive agriculture and then on to wage labor (Pérez Lizaur 1977).[1] The villages in the plains were the most advanced in this process for two reasons. First, being closer to Mexico City and Texcoco they had earlier access to services such as electricity and medical care that led to an earlier decrease in the mortality rate. And second, with less access to land and water for irrigation, with the population increase they were forced to shift more rapidly to intensive cultivation and then to wage labor. Meanwhile, the villages in the sierra, with a later demographic shift and access to more land and irrigation water, had only just recently begun the shift to intensive agriculture. The villages in the foothills, meanwhile, occupied an intermediate position, with a population density between that of the plains and the sierra and with a predominance of intensive agriculture giving way to wage labor.

More than thirty years after the publication of Pérez Lizaur's study, these kinds of conclusions regarding the three subregions still hold true to an extent. In comparison to the villages in the foothills, those in the sierra display a more disperse settlement pattern and more agricultural production, both intensive and extensive. An analogous contrast can be drawn between the villages of the foothills and those of the plains: in the plains, the settlement pattern is quite dense, to the extent that most observers would probably categorize it as "urban," and there is very little agriculture; in the foothills, we still find a settlement pattern dispersed enough to allow some agricultural production, mostly of the intensive sort.

With the continued advance of this process in the foothills and the sierra, however, the differences between the three subregions have become less marked. Since the 1970s, population density and employment in wage labor in the sierra and in the foothills has increased while agricultural production has decreased (Castro Pérez 2006:307–8; Pérez Lizaur 1977). It is important to note, however, that these changes are not attributable solely to population increase but also, and perhaps more importantly in recent years, to a decline in prices for crops (in particular, corn, with the end of government subsidies in the 1990s) and an improvement in transportation infrastructure (in particular, the completion of a highway across the Texcoco Lake bed in 1994) making wage labor in other parts of the region, such as Texcoco and Chiconcuac (see below), and in Mexico City more accessible.

In the same manner that the principal indicator of the rural—agricultural production—has severely declined throughout the region, the usual indicator of indigenousness—language, in this case Nahuatl—has also nearly disappeared, with the exception of the oldest generation of residents in the sierra villages. This change is in part due to the federal government's nationwide assimilation policies during the middle decades of the twentieth century, which attempted to more fully integrate indigenous people into the nation by converting them into Spanish-speaking mestizos. Schools were the main vehicle for this change, and children were punished, often cruelly, for speaking indigenous languages in class. In the case of the Texcoco region, villagers themselves adopted the goal of wanting their children to speak Spanish without an accent to shield them from the stigma of indigenousness and thus to improve their opportunities for education and work in the nearby cities. This strategy has proven successful, and the earnings from work in the city have facilitated the improvement of schools in the village, leading to further success in formal education and wage labor.

Regional Isolation and Deurbanization

At the same time that the region appears urban and mestizo in a number of ways, it has also remained relatively isolated, depopulated, and deurbanized. When I refer to the region's relatively low population density, I am comparing it to other areas on Mexico City's outskirts, such as Ecatepec or Xochimilco, which experienced a dramatic increase in population during the 1960s, 1970s, and 1980s. Texcoco was spared this transformation by its relative isolation caused by the barrier of the dry lakebed. When the toll highway spanning the lakebed was opened in 1994, Mexico City's period of rapid growth, mainly due to rural-urban migration, had basically ended. So while an increasing number of people from the city have migrated to the region in recent years, it has not experienced the kind of dramatic transformation that has occurred in other periurban regions of the Valley of Mexico.

This relative isolation from the urban sprawl has also meant that the region has continued to exist as such, at least in a certain sense. The Texcoco region is hardly isolated in comparison to many others in Mexico's highlands and has probably not been self-sufficient, in the sense of supplying its own food, since the 1930s. While many people in the region continue to produce corn for consumption, they no longer sell to nonproducers in the region, who have access to cheaper, industrially produced corn or other foodstuffs from elsewhere.[2] This process began in the postrevolutionary period when the Mexican government invested heavily in infrastructure for agro-industry in other parts of the country (Castro Pérez 2006:305–6) and then continued in the neoliberal period with the opening of the Mexican market to inexpensive corn from the United States. Both of these periods also saw improvements in transportation with the midcentury construction of the Mexico City–Veracruz highway that passes through the region and then the completion of a toll highway across the lakebed in 1994. However, despite this lack of isolation and self-sufficiency, residents continue to recognize the region as a region. And even though they have numerous connections to people in Mexico City through school or work-related activities, most of their social relations with people from outside their own village are with residents of the region's other communities. For example, when people marry outside their own village, it is usually with someone from another village in the region. They also occasionally form ritual kinship relations with people from one of the other villages. These relations become apparent during a village's fiesta for the patron saint when its residents prepare to receive their in-laws, cousins, and *compadres* (co-godparents) from other villages. The fiestas themselves involve other types of connections among villages in the region. Sometimes the members of one community maintain a relationship with another's patron saint, exchanging participation in the fiesta for the saint's blessing and protection. The region's residents also say that they take the saints, in the form of images, to "visit" neighboring villages.

The region is also constituted by a division of labor through which residents of different villages supply each other with certain products, services, and sources of employment. This division of labor among communities began in prehispanic times, when it also included food production, consumption, and exchange. As I mentioned above, the region is no longer self-sufficient in terms of food production, and most of the goods consumed there are industrial products brought in from elsewhere. However, the division of labor remains in a reduced form. Much of what is produced and exchanged in different villages is consumed in fiestas: flowers, clay cooking pots, fireworks, and musical groups. The village that used to supply wool clothing, Chiconcuac, is now a center for the *maquila* (assembly) and production of clothing, with importance at an international level (see below). Thus, Chiconcuac currently occupies a key role in this division of labor, supplying employment to people throughout the region.

When I say that the region has remained relatively deurbanized, I am referring to the fact that the city of Texcoco lacks importance as a political, economic, or cultural center in comparison to other cities that are also close to the capital, such as Toluca and Pachuca, which were less important than Texcoco as urban centers in the prehispanic period but are now state capitals. I think that this deurbanization can be explained in the same manner that Bonfil Batalla (1973) describes the situation of the city of Cholula. This city was an important urban center in the prehispanic period, but instead of establishing a regional capital there, the Spanish built a new capital city, Puebla, nearby. According to Bonfil Batalla, the existence of Puebla obviated the need for political, economic, or cultural services in Cholula. Thus, while the city of Cholula did not disappear, its importance as an urban center basically did. Similarly, Texcoco's proximity to Mexico City, combined with the decision to make Toluca and not Texcoco the State of Mexico's capital, meant that Texcoco declined in importance as an urban center. While the region's residents have access to some political, economic, or cultural services in Texcoco, for many other things they must travel to Mexico City or Toluca. Bonfil Batalla uses the example of Cholula to question the validity of Robert Redfield's (1970 [1941]) idea that urbanization is a product of proximity to a city, occurring through a process of diffusion. As long as we understand urban development as the creation of a political, economic, or cultural center, the opposite appears to be the case, he claims, since these services are more essential in cities that are distant from important urban centers. Palerm and Wolf (1972) make a similar argument using the Texcoco region as their example. These authors use the categories of "key" versus "marginal" areas instead of speaking of the urban and rural. They argue that the intensive agricultural production that made the region a key area in the fifteenth century marginalized it after the conquest, in a new society organized around other kinds of productive activities. I would add that the region has remained marginal in recent years despite the increase of nonagricultural activities such as the production of clothing (see below) since these latter activities still occupy a secondary role in the broader economy.

One consequence of this deurbanization is that while the city undoubtedly plays a central role in people's lives, the lack of development of political, economic, and cultural institutions in the region has meant that people have not totally lost control of their lives and their future because of pressures from external powers. This situation of deurbanization, in which the world of the city is present and accessible but, at the same time, at a safe distance, has meant that the region's residents have, in many cases, been able to incorporate new practices from the city in a selective manner. In other words, instead of being forcibly urbanized, which, I think, is how we usually imagine indigenous people's or peasants' relation to the urban, they have exercised control or agency in the process. As I discuss in more detail in chapter 5, many residents see the urban or the modern neither as a threat or a salvation but rather as a source of new ways of improving their lives at the community, family, or individual level.

Beyond "Urban" versus "Rural" and "Mestizo" versus "Indigenous"

I would like to return briefly to the differences among the subregions, which continue to exist to an extent alongside of region-wide processes of urbanization and deurbanization. I believe it is important to address the fact that they look a lot like Redfield's (1970 [1941]) folk-urban continuum. For example, such a continuum is apparently evidenced by the fact that the shift from agriculture to wage labor is more advanced as one travels from the sierra to the plains, and also that population density increases as we move in this direction. Also fitting the pattern of this continuum is the fact that the shift in language from Nahuatl to Spanish has occurred more recently in the sierra than in the foothills and more recently in the foothills than in the plains. Additionally, there is an idea shared among the residents of the region that as one moves from the plains to the sierra that the communities tend to have retained more of their "traditions," by which they mean things such as beliefs in supernatural beings and the use of traditional healers. And as in Redfield's formulation, I would say that the reason for these differences undoubtedly has something to do with proximity or distance from the city.

However, despite the apparent applicability of Redfield's theory, we should avoid the temptation of assuming that this formulation can fully explain the processes of change in the region and its relationship to the city. Alongside the differences among the villages in the subregions mentioned above, the manners of understanding, being, and acting in the world described in the following three chapters appear to be found fairly consistently through the region. For example, fiestas and mayordomías throughout the region revolve around what I refer to as the production of active subjects (see, e.g., Encarnación Ruiz 2004; López Millán 2008; Rodríguez Hernández 2008), and people from villages in all three subregions insist on distinguishing themselves from "city people." I would even say that the people in the plains are perhaps the most vehement in doing so. One possible interpretation of this is that it has to do with identity in the sense that they feel the need to distinguish themselves precisely because they are similar to city people. However, I do not believe that this is the case: the people of plains villages do not display any such identity crisis, nor have I heard of people in the foothills or sierra accusing them of being like city people. Instead, I would say that because of their proximity to the city, they have benefited the most from what it has to offer in know-how, technology, and so forth, but at the same time, they are the most conscious of the differences between themselves and city people, and they have been the most frequently threatened by urban development projects. As I explain further in chapter 5, the threat is not urban "culture" in and of itself but, rather, actors and projects that intend to extend their power over the region's residents.

The "Indigenousness" of the Plains Villages: Atenco and the Airport

One example of this vehement reaction from a plains village against external projects brought nationwide attention to the Texcoco region and fame or infamy, depending on the position taken, to the village of San Salvador Atenco. In 2001, the government attempted to purchase Atenco's *ejidal* lands,[3] located principally in the dry lakebed, with the intention of constructing on them a new international airport for Mexico City. Village residents, or at least a good number of them, not only refused the offer but also organized to protest and to block the construction of the airport. They claimed that they were not interested in selling these lands that their ancestors had fought for in the Revolution and that they were opposed to the flood of development and urbanization that the construction of the airport would bring. This second worry was shared by many residents of villages throughout the region, who feared that the airport would bring a flood of urban development, which would lead to significant ecological and sociocultural changes. The beginning of construction to widen and improve the highway that runs through the region on its way to Tlaxcala and eventually to Veracruz foretold of such plans to open the region to urban expansion at a new and faster pace.

In the initial stages of Atenco's opposition, the government continued to push the sale on the village residents, but after a few confrontations between protesters and authorities brought national media attention, the government backed down and cancelled their plans.[4] A resident of Tepetlaoxtoc, whose work as a government liaison to local *ejido* commissions had brought him into contact with people from Atenco, told me that it did not surprise him at all that Atenco's residents had opposed the airport and had done so successfully. He explained that Atenco's residents had, on the basis of numerous experiences, developed a strong distrust of and opposition to government projects. He added that with the region's division of labor among villages, Atenco had recently taken on the role of defender and protester. An example of Atenco taking on this role within the region occurred in 2006 when a group of flower vendors from the sierra village of Santa Catarina asked Atenco for help in defending their right to sell in public spaces in Texcoco.[5]

The federal government's failure to negotiate successfully with Atenco's residents is at least partly the result of erroneous assumptions similar to those found in Redfield's formulation about the category "urban." As I mention above, Atenco, like most other plains villages, would appear to an outside observer to be "urban" because of the dense settlement pattern, the paved streets and other "modern" services, and the relative lack of agricultural production. This last feature of villages such as Atenco, right on the shore of the lakebed, is attributed not only to population density and lack of irrigation but also to the salinity of the lakebed soil. Government officials, working with this assumption of Atenco's having been incorporated into Mexico City's urban sprawl, not unsurprisingly believed that Atenco's residents would see their agricultural land as a commodity and an almost useless commodity at that. Additionally, they imagined that the region's residents would appreciate the urban development and the jobs that would become available with the airport's construction and operation. We could even say that the classification of Atenco as urban rather than indigenous makes the village's residents so ordinary as to become invisible. I once came across an exhibit of the plans for the airport's construction. The representations of what the area would look like after the construction of the airport along with accompanying ecological renewal efforts, including the re-creation of the lake, were colorful and inspiring but completely omitted any mention of the region's residents. To the architects who designed the project, the region's residents were basically inexistent.

In Mexico, indigenous communities' ability to organize and act collectively to protect their interests is recognized and even feared by the government. In fact, we could say that the state's efforts to modernize indigenous people and integrate them into the nation were and are, in part, motivated by a desire to break down these powerful collectivities. But in the case of Atenco, the government's and others' classification of Atenco as urban and mestizo, or in some cases inexistent, blinded them to the possibility that the village's residents might react in this collective manner. It also blinded officials to the possibility that the residents did not see their land as a commodity and that they could be opposed to urban development. The costs of this blindness were multiplied by the fact that Atenco's residents were predisposed to question and reject government projects and other types of external impositions. We could say that the example of Atenco's successful opposition to the airport provides a clear example of the pitfalls of applying a folk-urban continuum to the region's subregions. I would add that easily observable differences among the subregions should not distract us from similarities that categories such as "urban," "rural," "mestizo," and "indigenous" can blind us to. As I have already mentioned, my main argument here is not about such categorizations, but I do believe that they can distract us, and that they have distracted us, from the practices that I call attention to in the following chapters.

The Village of Tepetlaoxtoc

The village where I conducted research, Tepetlaoxtoc, or Tepetlaoxtoc de Hidalgo, as it is officially known, is about twelve kilometers northeast of Texcoco and forty-two kilometers northeast of Mexico City's center. It is the *cabecera*, or seat of a municipality of the same name, that, like the

Figure 2.1 The center of Tepetlaoxtoc, 2004.

municipality of Texcoco just to the south, extends from the plains up into the sierra. The village of Tepetlaoxtoc houses approximately six thousand inhabitants and the municipality about nineteen thousand. The rest of the population is distributed among six other villages and numerous smaller settlements situated throughout the municipality.

The village is divided into a *centro* (center) and seven *barrios* (a traditional neighborhood division). Each barrio has a chapel housing a patron saint, for whom a fiesta is celebrated. The center houses both a large parish church dedicated to Santa María Magdalena and another smaller church dedicated to San Sebastián, the patron saint of the entire village. Villagers will always give priority to San Sebastián and his fiesta, putting them before María Magdalena and the barrios' saints. I observed that villagers give little importance to the division into barrios and in fact sometimes downplay it by stating that they are all part of the same community and that they all participate in all of the fiestas. Even the saints participate in all of the fiestas, because they are physically taken to "visit" their fellow saints on the latter's "day."[6]

Such statements are possibly made in reference to an earlier period when the division into barrios was more significant. A couple of villagers explained to me that during the 1950s and 1960s, there were frequent

Figure 2.2 A street near the center of Tepetlaoxtoc, 2011.

fights, often resulting in fatalities, between young men from the different barrios. The violence was finally quelled when a municipal president requested that the army occupy the village for a few weeks. I do not know what underlying economic or political divisions, if any, caused these confrontations, but it seems fairly clear that on a personal level these confrontations had to do with people "acting big," in the terms of James Taggart's informants (2007:54), or being *presumido* (conceited), in those of my own. Villagers today associate such attitudes with the pernicious individualistic greed and obsession with accumulation linked to the city and to capitalism. Villagers' downplaying of the distinctions among barrios likely constitutes, on a specific level, a continued effort to close the divisions that arose during this period of conflict and, on a more general level, to reject the individualism of the city in favor of interdependence. Taggart (2007:73–82) describes an analogous effort in Huitzilan, Puebla: after a brutally violent conflict between two factions raged for nearly a decade, villagers succeeded in "healing" the social wounds through rituals that emphasized "fastening" and "sewing" people together. Taggart explains that women took on leading roles in these rituals; women in Tepetlaoxtoc also lead the way in emphasizing solidarity at the village level.

Tepetlaoxtoc is one of those villages in the region that complicates the division into topographical subregions. It is located just below and quite close to the string of villages in the foothills but is different from these villages in that it lacks water for irrigation and a significant extension of ejidal lands for agricultural production (Pérez Lizaur 1977). Thus, although its location and altitude suggest that it would be similar to the foothills villages, it really has more in common with the plains villages, sharing their denser settlement pattern, the near disappearance of agricultural activities, and their earlier loss of the Nahuatl language.

Changing Economic Activities

The village's role as a center of political power in relation to the surrounding settlements dates back to prehispanic times. During colonial times the village also gained economic importance as a stopping point along the road running from Veracruz on the gulf coast to Mexico City. Many villagers worked as *arrieros* (mule drivers) during this period, and the village housed an important regional market. With the construction of a railway line at the close of the nineteenth century, however, these activities all but disappeared. The railway line passed just a few kilometers from Tepetlaoxtoc, but Tepetlaoxtoc's economic importance as a stopover point for long-distance travelers declined in any case, and then declined further still with the construction of a highway in the mid-twentieth century that bypassed the village. With the loss of these economic activities, Tepetlaoxtoc's position as municipal center in relation to the surrounding communities was reduced to its political aspect.[7] Today, the residents of the municipality's other villages are drawn instead to Mexico City, Texcoco, or other villages in the region such as Chiconcuac (see below) in their activities as producers and consumers.

During the colonial period and up to the Revolution of 1910, nearby haciendas, principally devoted to raising cattle and sheep, denied Tepetlaoxtoc's residents access to agricultural land and to water for irrigation (Campos de García 1973). As a consequence, many villagers served as workers on these haciendas (Campos de García 1973; Pérez Lizaur 1977). Others produced pulque and transported it to Texcoco,[8] but this activity has steadily declined since the middle of the twentieth century as industrially produced bottled alcoholic beverages have come to dominate the urban and rural consumer markets. Residents also produced corn, mostly for their own consumption, but this also declined at midcentury because of an increase in population, which limited access to agricultural land and to water for irrigation from a now-dry underground river, as well as the introduction of cheaper foodstuffs from other parts of the country (Castro Pérez 2006:305–6). In response to the mid-twentieth-century decline in local production of pulque and corn coupled with improvements in transportation due to the new highway, villagers began migrating in significant numbers to Mexico City to find work. Villagers generally considered these migrations to be temporary and returned to the village on a weekly basis or periodically for celebrations such as the fiestas for the patron saints. This was a period of rapid economic growth in Mexico, and thus villagers had little trouble finding work or starting small businesses and then bringing in relatives to work with them. The first generation of migrants often worked as domestic servants, as employees in markets and restaurants, or as artisans such as carpenters and painters. The next generation, whose members in many cases received some secondary education in the city because their parents worked there, moved, in many cases, into the rapidly expanding industrial or public sectors. In the 1970s and 1980s, many of these villagers held apparently stable and well-paying jobs in unionized factories, public schools, and government offices. During this period the village was somewhat of a ghost town, with most people living and working in Mexico City. Within the region, Tepetlaoxtoc was somewhat unique in this sense because it lacked the agricultural opportunities of the foothills and sierra villages, and also the proximity of the plains villages, which allowed more easily for a daily commute to the city.

As a consequence of a series of national economic crises and neoliberal remedies throughout the 1980s and 1990s, many of these villagers lost these stable, well-paying jobs. In response, many people moved back to the village to live rent-free on inherited land. With this return migration, the village came back to life. Many residents talk about this moment of revival in terms of the growth in size and importance of the fiestas for patron saints. In fact, many aspects of the specific form of the fiestas and mayordomías that I describe in the following chapter originated quite recently, in the 1980s. Returning to the subject of economic activities, some of these return migrants have taken advantage of the newly completed highway crossing the Texcoco Lake bed to commute to Mexico City on a daily basis for work or, in the case of a few, for study at the university level.[9] Even with the new highway, however, the commute is a long one. Villagers must take a local bus from Tepetlaoxtoc to Texcoco, an express bus to one of Mexico City's bus stations, and then the subway or another bus or buses to reach their final destination. Just to get to Mexico City's bus station, the trip takes an

Figure 2.3 The church of San Sebastián, Tepetlaoxtoc's principal patron saint, 2011.

hour and a half to two hours and costs about twenty-five pesos each way.[10] Villagers explained to me that they put up with the commute not so much for the amount they can make in jobs in the city but rather because of the benefits such as medical care and retirement pensions they receive. Many villagers own cars or pickup trucks, but most do not use them for commuting on a daily basis, because of the cost of gasoline and the thirty-peso toll on the Texcoco–Mexico City highway. Others have taken up new activities within the village or region, often using their severance pay or pensions from jobs in the city to get started. The three most common activities taken up were cattle "fattening," construction work, and the *maquila* (assembly) of clothes.

Cattle fattening consists of buying one-year-old cattle, feeding them for three months until they are ready to be butchered, and then selling them directly to a slaughterhouse or to a middleman. This industry has taken off following its success in the neighboring village of Jolalpan, where some villagers have acquired as many as a thousand head.[11] While the residents of Tepetlaoxtoc rarely go to Jolalpan to work as salaried laborers, the middlemen whom they buy from and sell to are often from the latter village. So even though Tepetlaoxtoc's fatteners see themselves as independent businessmen, they are, in reality, working indirectly for Jolalpan's middlemen. Success in Tepetlaoxtoc is quite variable. Some have been able to acquire as many as one hundred head, while others cannot get past ten. "Fatteners" generally want to increase their volume because this means higher profits. The problem is that this requires an initial investment that not everyone can make, although most aspire to. Impediments include the start-up costs of constructing a large corral and then the initial payment for the year-old calves and their feed. There are also risks: if the cattle get sick and die, the whole investment is lost. Fatteners who have managed to accumulate forty head are considered to be truly successful. At this point it becomes necessary and advantageous to hire an employee, which further increases their profits and potential for growth.

I suspect that this industry has taken off in the region in recent years because of its proximity to Mexico City. The cattle, which are bred on large ranches in Veracruz, can be transported most of the way to Mexico City before reaching their maximum weight, to save on shipping costs. Once a few people in this region achieved success, the knowledge of how to do the fattening and of the potential for success was passed around to family members, friends, and neighbors, leading to the spread and growth of this activity. The current price of the meat also makes it a fit for villagers in relation to what they could earn otherwise. If the price were higher, it is likely that they would be bumped out of the industry by others in a wealthier economic niche who could better compete with higher investments; if it were lower, villagers would give it up for other activities, and it would become available to others in lower economic niches. As an example of the precariousness of such economic activities, one informant explained to me that in the 1970s and 1980s, pig fattening was a popular activity, but when cheaper pork was introduced from the United States around 1985, forcing prices down, most gave it up, which is not to say that people have given up this activity throughout Mexico.

Construction work takes place mostly in the village and region and ranges from minor jobs such as building "stalls" for small businesses such as stores to larger, multiple-story structures such as weekend homes for wealthy urbanites to public works projects such as roads. In this industry, there is a three-tiered hierarchy with *ayudantes* or *chalanes* (helpers or assistants) at the bottom, *maestros* or *albañiles* (construction workers) in the middle, and contractors on top. The first two receive weekly salaries, and the contractors are paid by the job. Contractors themselves usually work as albañiles alongside of their employees, and on small jobs they may even do the work of helpers. Helpers and masters usually aspire to be masters and contractors, respectively, although some seem to recognize the limits of their ability and knowledge and admit that a move up the scale could be a problem for them. Employees receive no social security benefits, and the work is irregular—that is, a contractor hires his employees for a specific job without incurring any further commitment, even though they usually hire back the same people, who are generally friends or acquaintances from the village. There are also a few migrants working as helpers in the village who come from poorer rural areas of Mexico and from Central America.

Despite this potential for instability, jobs are regularly available, although, as one person complained, "There is always work, but the problem is that it doesn't pay enough." One source of funds for these construction projects is the weekenders from Mexico City. Another is the villagers who have managed to keep their jobs in the city and hire friends and family members still in the village to build residences and small businesses. A third source consists of people who lost jobs in Mexico City and have used their pensions, severance payments, or profits from local businesses to build or add onto residences and those businesses (building a corral, for example). All of these sources of funds for building projects are fairly recent—the past thirty or forty years—and thus, like the cattle fattening, the rise of the local construction industry is recent and at least indirectly a result of economic crises and neoliberal reforms. This flow of cash to the region could easily dry up or at least decrease if severance payments run out, if more villagers lose their jobs in the city, or if other local small industries such as cattle fattening begin to struggle with increased competition from elsewhere.

The maquila of clothes in the village, meanwhile, must be understood in reference to the plains village of Chiconcuac, which has gained importance over the past forty years as an economic center for residents throughout the region. Until the late 1970s, Chiconcuac participated in the region's division of labor as a producer of wool and knitted garments. Since then, the village has grown in importance as a center for the production, sale, and distribution of clothing of all sorts. In the late 1970s, residents of Chiconcuac began purchasing industrially produced fabrics and "assembling" (*maquilando*) them into garments in small family workshops, selling them in a weekly market, principally to wholesale buyers from Mexico City. Subsequently, the workshops grew and villagers from Chiconcuac began hiring workers from other villages in the region; more recently, they have begun to establish workshops in other villages or to outsource the assembly to family workshops in other villages. Furthermore, the market in Chiconcuac has turned into a center for distribution of clothing at a national and even international level with sellers and buyers from elsewhere meeting there to exchange their products. It could be said, in fact, that the region's economic center is no longer Texcoco but rather Chiconcuac, and the ties created by the clothing industry rather than the irrigation system are what constitute the region as such (see Pérez Lizaur and Zamora Wasserman 2010).

Like people from most other villages in the region, some of Tepetlaoxtoc's residents are employed in workshops in Chiconcuac, while in other cases they do maquila work in their home village. In the latter case, the workshop is usually but not necessarily owned by someone from Tepetlaoxtoc, but a middleman from Chiconcuac brings already-cut fabric to be sewn together in the workshop and then collects the finished product. Small workshops with just one or two sewing machines are operated by family members, while bigger ones hire employees to do some or most of the sewing. The biggest workshops I came across in Tepetlaoxtoc employ about ten people. As with the cattle fattening and the construction, most participants aspire to own their own workshops and machines and to increase volume so as to make it necessary and profitable to hire others. Not surprisingly, many do not achieve these goals. Again, in a manner similar to cattle fattening and construction, the region's clothing industry occupies a precarious position in the global economy and could easily be displaced by competition from elsewhere.

This brief chapter hardly does justice to the complex processes of economic change occurring in the region, and I have not even touched on a variety of other topics that would be necessary to achieve anything like a comprehensive understanding of residents' lives. My intention here is simply to give a brief description of life in the village of Tepetlaoxtoc and in the region as a whole to provide a concrete setting for the more specific discussions in the next three chapters.

"La fiesta se hace entre todos"

Rethinking Fiestas and Cargos

From the 1950s until well into the 1980s, the topic of cargo systems was central to anthropological work on highland Mesoamerican villages. Eric Wolf's (1955) writings on the closed corporate peasant community are usually seen as having initiated this trend even though cargo systems were not the primary focus in his work. Instead, his proposal was primarily aimed at questioning earlier assumptions that indigenous villages displayed a sort of timeless continuation of prehispanic culture. He suggested that indigenous people could be better understood as peasants, producing for a national and international market, with different structural relationships to those markets depending on the type of community in which they live. Wolf notes that in highland Latin America, the prehispanic and then the Spanish rulers encouraged the closing of peasant communities to facilitate a system of indirect rule and exploitation. He proposed the concept of the closed corporate community to describe these typical highland peasant villages. He then went on to describe how the peasants have since taken on the maintenance of this closed corporate community structure themselves, as a sort of cultural defense against the outside world. He suggested that one of the ways in which they maintain this structure is through the civil-religious cargo system installed by the Spanish. Pressure to spend in the system channels resources toward community-oriented consumption instead of capitalist development and individual conspicuous consumption. Furthermore, participation in the system defines membership in the community, marking and constantly reestablishing its boundaries.

Although his objective was to use this concept to describe a particular structural relationship between the peasants and the outside world, most subsequent authors were less interested in his broader comparison to other peasant types than in his conceptualization of the kind of highland indigenous communities that dominated anthropological studies of Mexico. It could be said that Wolf's notion of the closed corporate community and, in particular, of the cargo system's role in the production or reproduction of this community structure became a gatekeeping[1] topic in Mesoamerican anthropology.

Frank Cancian's (1965) frequently cited study of the cargo system in Zinacantán, in highland Chiapas, is exemplary in this sense. He posits, "The cargo system is crucial to the continued existence of Zinacantán as an Indian community, a community separate and distinct from its Ladino environment. Among the functions of the cargo system are: definition of the limits of community membership, reinforcement of commitment to common values, reduction of potential conflict, and support of traditional kinship patterns" (1965:133). According to Cancian, the cargo system creates the boundary that defines the community and is the glue that holds it together. Furthermore, it produces the hierarchical positions that constitute the community's internal social structure: "The cargo system ranks the members of the community into a single social structure. All sectors of the community accord prestige and respect to the incumbent and past cargo-holder, and the public nature of cargo service makes it an effective way of ranking all Zinacantecos" (1965:135). Cancian's attention to prestige introduced another enduring focus in studies of cargo systems: why individuals take on cargos (literally, "loads") even though they involve such a great expenditure of time and wealth. People take on this "load" either because they are obligated or pressured to do so by village leaders or because they volunteer, which they do to move up in the village's hierarchical social structure and/or to gain prestige. Thus, generally speaking, cargos were considered to be about individuals doing service for the community and in return gaining prestige and position in the village hierarchy. In other words, they were taken to be about the production of two different *things*: community (or social structure) and prestige. Some authors, such as Wolf, placed more emphasis on the former and others, such as Cancian, on the latter, although most seemed to recognize the importance of both motives.

These conclusions regarding cargo systems came to constitute the unquestioned base of Mesoamerican community studies. Debates that occurred did so on top of this base, for example, as regarding whether or not the cargo system, with its heavy expenditures, prevented socioeconomic stratification and the formation of classes. Other studies focused on a range of topics related to the cargo system and community structure, exploring their history (Chance and Taylor 1985; Rus and Wasserstrom 1980), variation over time (DeWalt 1975), the role of women (Mathews 1985), and their relationship to the broader political economy (Greenberg 1981), to name just a few examples.

By the 1990s, interest had begun to wane. I think there are two reasons for this. First, there occurred a shift of focus, following disciplinary trends, from structure to agency. Different topics, mostly related to questions of power and politics, came to the fore, including gender (Speed, Hernández Castillo, and Stephen 2006; Stephen 1991), identity (Friedlander 1975; Kearney 1996), migration (Cohen 2004; Rouse 1992), and social movements (Speed 2007; Stephen 2002). This shift from a focus on structure to one on agency, however, did not include an effort to think critically about how, if at all, our informants might think of such categories and the relationship between them.

The other reason why anthropologists' interest in cargo systems and community structure began to decline is simply that many researchers were finding that their informants were likewise losing interest. Eileen Mulhare, in her literature review of Mesoamerican social organization, is led to conclude, "Popular support for cargo systems in general is declining" (2000:21). Explanations for this decline usually relate to the penetration of the outside world into the community in the form of new ways of spending time and money: capitalist investments, education, and different religions (Mulhare 2000). Even if the fiestas and mayordomías did not disappear completely with these changes, the decline in interest was evidenced by "cost-sharing" systems, which emerged to allow the continuation of community celebrations despite declining interest (Brandes 1981, 1988; Cohen 1999; DeWalt 1975; Smith 1977). In such systems, mayordomos were expected to only collect money or other goods from fellow villages for the fiesta instead of having to fund it themselves. Not surprisingly, since the cargo system was equated with community structure and the outside world is assumed to be constituted by individualism and factionalism—community's opposites—there were reports that community was declining as well. For example, Cancian, in his restudy of Zinacantán, concludes, "Community declined in Zinacantán between the early 1960's and the early 1980's" (1992:201). So after numerous anthropologists decided that we had been giving too much attention to structure at the expense of agency, and considering that structure was disappearing from these communities in any case, the topic was pretty much dropped, at least by anthropologists publishing primarily in English. My concern here is not the fact that it was dropped, and by no means am I arguing simply for a return to the study of cargo systems. Rather, I think that we may have dropped it for the wrong reasons. That is, it was dropped because of the broader disciplinary shift in interest to agency without a critical examination of the notion that cargos were about structure to begin with. Thus, anthropologists may have misinterpreted what was really going on with cargos, fiestas, and community and consequently may not have really understood the significance, or lack thereof, of their supposed disappearance. In other words, the focus on the structural or systemic aspects of cargo systems and community may have distracted anthropologists from other manners in which these practices are important to the people we study. For example, Cancian recognizes that cargo holders in Zinacantán are expected to involve others: "[I]t is considered normal and proper to borrow about half the money needed for a cargo" (1965:100; my emphasis). Similarly, Robert Laughlin notes that it was usual for mayordomos in Zinacantán to coax monetary donations from others: "But most tedious of all was the statement, 'I want to talk to you,' which invariably was followed by the request for a loan, which customarily would be given to religious officials without interest" (2010:47). However, neither author pursues the significance of these "customs" and instead reduces them to simple financial concerns: "loans." Because the study of cargos was dropped completely as part of the move away from structure and system, there has been no attempt to get beyond the structure/system distraction and find out whether these practices are important to our informants in manners unrelated to structure and system that might still remain after their decline or disappearance.

I suggest, based on my findings in Tepetlaoxtoc, that we were right all along that something important was going on with the cargos, but it is not the cargos themselves or the structure produced by them. Rather, we could say that the cargos provide a structure as a kind of starting point or base on which people can produce each other as active subjects. The cargos and the related structure are means to an end and not ends in themselves. People in Tepetlaoxtoc, instead of sharing our preoccupation with the production of things such as community and prestige, are interested in producing action in others. The mayordomo, for example, does not put on the fiesta himself, making an individual sacrifice for the community. Rather, he causes other people's participation, so that the fiesta *se hace entre todos* (is put on by everybody).

It could even be said that this decline of cargo systems, or at least of their structural-hierarchical facet, permitted nonstructural, action-oriented aspects of cargos to come to the fore in highland villages and in anthropologists' more recent descriptions. Saúl Millán (2005), for example, stresses horizontal relations constituted by the circulation of cargos and prestations. Jeffrey Cohen (1999), meanwhile, focuses on the practice of "cooperation" at the family and community level in a Zapotec Oaxacan village. John Monaghan (1990), working in a Mixtec Oaxacan village, argues that exchanges of tortillas during fiestas are not just a means but an end in themselves, and while they may be important as redistribution, their real significance lies in people's actions and not in the things exchanged in and of themselves. Catharine Good Eshelman (2004a) describes how in Nahua communities in the state of Guerrero, "working together" is central to how people understand fiestas and other community activities. She quotes a cargo holder: "My first thought as an authority is: How are we going to make ourselves into one? How are we going to work all together? How can I achieve making us one? If someone doesn't want to accompany us, we'll try to look for a way so that he unites with us, so that he helps us also" (2004a:147; my translation).

Tepetlaoxtoc, as I have already suggested, offers a particularly clear view of these action-oriented aspects of cargos not only because of the absence of a domineering civil-religious hierarchy but also because its proximity to Mexico City has led residents to make explicit these local understandings of action in opposition to their urban counterparts. Other anthropologists working in communities close to or within Mexico City, Puebla, and other major urban centers have similarly found that cargo systems and fiestas play a key role in representing and reproducing a local or indigenous value system or worldview in response to urban expansion. This trend can be traced to Guillermo Bonfil Batalla's (1973) study of Cholula, in which he attempts to explain how and why this "sacred city's" residents have maintained their indigenousness despite their integration into the industrial capitalist economy and their proximity to Puebla, a major urban center. He posits that residents, who neither speak an indigenous language nor outwardly claim an indigenous identity, have actively conserved an unnamed indigenousness in the fiestas and cargo systems, in part because these practices provide an alternative route to prestige for those relegated to the margins of urban life. More recently, María Ana Portal Ariosa (1997) and Andrés Medina Hernández (2007), writing about villages in Tlalpan in the southern part of the Federal District, claim that residents' creativity and the potential for flexibility in the organization of cargos and fiestas have allowed them to preserve a local worldview and identity in the face of repression from urban actors interested in exploiting their land and labor.

For example, residents have democratized cargo systems in response to social and economic circumstances imposed by the city (Portal Ariosa 1997:177), but despite this transformation they continue to play a key role in the reproduction of local cultural values and identity (1997:143).

Tepetlaoxtoc's cargos and fiestas have undergone a similar process of breakdown and transformation brought about by local responses to urban influence over land and labor. From the 1940s to the 1970s, the village's residents were drawn to jobs in Mexico City's expanding economy. Import-substitution policies combined with political and economic centralization led to the rapid growth of industry and government bureaucracy in the nation's capital. The village became something of a ghost town as community members moved into the city to take on relatively high-paying, often unionized jobs. However, with the economic crises of the 1980s and '90s and the neoliberal reforms and budget cuts meant to resolve them, many of Tepetlaoxtoc's residents lost their jobs and returned to the village. The village came back to life, as did its cargos and fiestas. Up until the mid-1980s and back at least as far as the second quarter of the twentieth century, Tepetlaoxtoc's fiestas were put on by groups of residents denominated *compañías*.[2] While not exactly a civil-religious hierarchy, the *compañía* system, in ways similar to the *cofradía* system described by John Chance and William Taylor (1985), did involve a kind of hierarchical structure. Cargos in the different compañías associated with specific fiestas were consistently occupied by members of the same families, and some fiestas were considered more important and prestigious than others. While overall participation was hardly limited to an economic elite, the compañías undoubtedly represented an exclusionary practice, distinct from the possibility of upward mobility offered by the ladderlike civil-religious hierarchy. However, while the compañía system was even less democratic than a civil-religious hierarchy, it was also less individualistic: a principle of "doing things among everyone" was present even if "everyone" referred to an exclusive group.

Community members' earlier exodus from the village coupled with their mass return in the 1980s and 1990s offered an opportunity to "reinvent" (Portal Ariosa 1997:155) aspects of village life, in particular, the cargos and fiestas. As people returned from the city ready to renew their participation in village life, the exclusionary structure of the compañías was abandoned, while their internal organization of a mayordomo and a series of compañeros, or helpers, was expanded to include anyone willing to participate. The role of this group, referred to as *un equipo* (a team) also changed: instead of funding the fiesta themselves, they were expected not only to make a monetary contribution but also to precipitate and organize everybody else's participation. This new, more inclusive and more democratic manner of putting on the fiesta served to satisfy return migrants' desire for participation: although this system is apparently similar to the "cost-sharing" systems mentioned above, in the case of Tepetlaoxtoc, I was told that it emerged in reaction to *increased* interest in fiesta participation. This new manner of putting on the fiesta also coincided with an egalitarian ethic picked up in the city from a variety of different sources: the state-promoted ideals of the Mexican Revolution, the possibilities of upward economic mobility offered by a relatively free market, and the emerging multiparty democracy.

Yet this new manner of putting on the fiesta also arose in opposition to the individualism and materialism that villagers had experienced and disliked in the city. Thus, while they rejected the exclusionary structure of the old system, they breathed new life into the local ideal of "doing things among everyone." Through this ideal, they set up a contrast between urbanites' belief in individual agency and their own insistence on needing others, even to initiate an action. They also contrasted city people's obsession with things and possessions with their own nonpossessive valorization of people and their actions and subjective states. The significance of these contrasts was amplified by the fact that the city's individualism and materialism had followed them back to the village. On the one hand, urban migrants began to arrive looking for inexpensive housing, and on the other, the newly returned and unemployed villagers used their severance pay and business know-how acquired in the city to set up petty capitalist enterprises (see chapter 2). The unfortunate urban migrants and their inept attempts at participation in community practices came to represent all of the city's evil ways. Villagers, meanwhile, expressed discomfort with their new role in promoting an individualistic neoliberal model of hiring and letting go fellow villagers without providing them with any sort of job security or benefits. Thus, putting on the fiesta "among everyone" could be seen as a continued defense against the "city ways" and neoliberalism that people confront in their daily lives, although I think that one could say with equal accuracy that city ways and neoliberalism provide villagers with a contrast that facilitates their conceptualization of cargos and fiestas.

The Mayordomo as Motivator

As I have already stated, in contrast to the model in which the mayordomo or the mayordomo's family sponsors the fiesta, in Tepetlaoxtoc it primarily involves getting other people to *participar* (participate) or *cooperar* (cooperate). *Participar* is the more general term, used to refer to all action in the context of fiestas, while *cooperar* usually refers more specifically to the act of giving cash to the mayordomo; these donations are referred to as *cooperaciones*. These terms have specific meanings inseparable from the practices to which they refer in fiestas (and which I will describe below). Thus, we must be careful not to impose our own understandings of these terms derived from their use in other contexts. Once talking to someone in the village, I substituted the word *contribución* (contribution) for *cooperación*, assuming the two terms to be synonyms, and was swiftly corrected. I suspect that one or both of these terms (*participar* and *cooperar*) are translations from Nahuatl—perhaps even of the phrase "[S]an ce hueye tequitin" ("They work as one, one big one") noted by Good Eshelman (2004a:137). At least, I think, it is helpful to think of them as translations to maintain an open mind about their meanings.

Getting others involved begins with putting together un equipo (a team) of compañeros (companions). This "team" is the present version of the compañía that formerly sponsored the whole fiesta. Generally, three of the team members are given specific titles: *primer compañero, segundo compañero*, and *tercer compañero*, and the rest are just called compañeros and can include any number of people but usually count between twenty and fifty. Being one of these first three compañeros is considered to be almost equivalent to being a mayordomo, and when I asked people about the mayordomías they had done, many of them would also include in their list the times they had been one of this first group of compañeros. The mayordomo and all of the compañeros may cooperate with the same fixed sum, or the mayordomo and the first three compañeros may cooperate with more, while the rest of the compañeros give a somewhat lower, but also fixed, amount. This fixed sum can range from 1,500 to 5,000 pesos, depending on the size and importance of the fiesta. The fiestas for San Sebastián are more important and bigger than those of the barrios' saints, and there is also variation among the different mayordomías for San Sebastián.

The mayordomo and his first three compañeros each pay for a meal, supposedly for "everyone," even though the "everyone" turns out in practice to be mostly just the compañeros and the people who cooperated for the fiesta. The first compañero usually provides *una cena* (a supper) the night before; the second compañero, *un desayuno* (a breakfast) the day of the fiesta; the mayordomo, *la comida* (the large midafternoon meal) the day of the fiesta; and the third compañero, the supper on the *mero día* (the exact day of the fiesta). For a big fiesta, the mayordomo or the compañeros can spend as much as seventy thousand pesos on a meal, prepared for up to four thousand people. The smaller, barrio fiestas are for only about five hundred people and imply spending only about ten thousand to fifteen thousand pesos. These mayordomos or compañeros will usually receive "ayuda" from their parents, children, or siblings to pay for the meal, however (see chapter 4).

The mayordomo and his compañeros spend more money on the fiesta than does anybody else, but more significant than this individual spending is the idea that they are supposed to *trabajar* (work), and to do so as a team. The mayordomo and the first three compañeros are expected to do the most work and to coordinate the other compañeros the rest of the time. Most of the work involves going from house to house during the whole year leading up to the fiesta to collect cooperaciones. Often this means going to a house a few different times, since many people prefer to make a series of monthly payments because it is easier on their finances and also because it allows them to keep an eye on the mayordomo and his compañeros and make sure they are *trabajando* (working). The mayordomo and his compañeros are on the job during many other moments as well. For example, other fiestas during the year provide a good moment for trying to get people to give a cooperación or at least make a commitment to do so later on. They always carry around a notebook for writing down the commitments and a block of specially printed receipts for when they receive money.[3] In general, people say that you can see that a mayordomo is doing a good job if you see him going around "working," that is, taking up collections of cooperaciones, and villagers are more willing to give cooperaciones if they see the mayordomo and his team working in this manner. They say that there is not much point in giving to a mayordomo who is not getting many people to participate and thus will not put on a good fiesta.

The "team" also does other kinds of work, including ritual duties involving the saint and his church during the year leading up to the fiesta; the cleaning, decorating, and setting up that constitutes the preparation for the fiesta itself; and then some sort of improvement on the church, such as upkeep, adding on rooms, or adding pews or decorations. This last *obra* (work) is usually done after the fiesta, because it is supposed to be done with whatever funds are left over after the fiesta, even though everyone knows that money is supposed to be left over for just this purpose. Thus, to sum up (although I will return to certain details of this process at different moments in this chapter), a mayordomo does well by putting together a good team of compañeros, and the team does well by bringing about the participation of lots of other people.

Participation as Interdependent Action

By now, it should be becoming clear that when the people in Tepetlaoxtoc say "la fiesta se hace entre todos," they do not mean that they act as some sort of collective whole. Rather, there is an important division of labor in which certain people motivate others to act. In an attempt to describe to me what being a mayordomo is about, an informant once told me that the village is like a wheel: the compañeros are like the spokes and the other villagers the outer rim. Everyone is there and ready to cooperate, but they need the mayordomo to get things started by pushing the wheel so that it starts moving. In other words, it is not the community or its social structure that has to be produced, but rather action among its members.

This division of labor and the problem of getting others to act are present in just about all of the moments when someone gives a cooperación or decides to take on a cargo as mayordomo or compañero. When a mayordomo or compañero knocks on a door to ask for a cooperación, he gives a short but polite speech describing what the team plans to do for the fiesta and for the improvement of the church and then asks for the cooperación quite formally, often stating that they would be happy to accept any amount the potential donor would like to give. Before I had begun to understand the importance of this speech, there were a couple of occasions when, in my eagerness to receive invitations to fiestas, I reached into my pocket to prepare my cooperación as soon as someone approached me with their book of receipts. At the time, I attributed the uneasiness that my precipitous action produced to the reluctance of including an outsider in community practices. However, I later figured out that it was not my being an outsider but my odd behavior of acting on my own, before being invited to act, that produced this reaction.

Sometimes, however, this polite speech is not enough, and the potential donor will invite the mayordomo or compañero into his house and ask him to have a drink, perhaps saying, "If you have one tequila with me, I'll give you a hundred pesos . . . if you have two, I'll give you two hundred pesos," and so on. Being invited in for a drink may not sound that bad, but a mayordomo will consider this part of the strain of his work, which we can understand if we imagine the number of houses he has to visit.[4] The potential donor also sees this as making the mayordomo work, or in a sense, testing him to see whether he is willing to work to get cooperaciones and will thus put on a good fiesta by getting others to participate. Potential donors will also test the mayordomo and make him work by agreeing to give a cooperación but making him come back many times to collect all of it. As

I state earlier, this spacing out of the payment is easier on the finances of the donor, but this is not the only reason for doing so. And while I am talking about "tests" and this great effort on the part of the mayordomo to coax a cooperación out of the potential donor, I should add that the outcome of the whole interaction is in a certain sense already determined. The potential donor has reasons for giving a cooperación that have nothing to do with the mayordomo but rather with his relationship to the saint (discussed below). Furthermore, the mayordomo has in most cases knocked on that particular door because he gave a cooperación to the potential donor when the latter was mayordomo sometime in the past and he is coming back now to collect "his own money" (another topic described in fuller detail below). The fact that the mayordomo works so hard to convince someone of something that has already been determined sounds like a contradiction. However, I believe that it stops sounding this way when we take into account the fact that action is not supposed to emerge from an individual mind and will but instead must be induced by others. The wheel is already there, representing the relationships between the actors, including their debts, but the problem is to get it rolling. I find it useful to describe this approach to action as "interdependent," in contrast to our usual categorization of action into that which is independent versus that which demonstrates dependency or domination because it is a product of one person's control over another.

Another practice that involves interdependent action or the production of action in others is the passing of the mayordomía from one person to another. In most of the literature on cargo systems, mayordomos are appointed by a group of elders at the top of the civil-religious hierarchy. This happens either because the potential mayordomo has volunteered for the post and has been waiting on a list or because he has been shirking his community duties and thus the elders choose him. In many of the other villages in the Texcoco region there is a predetermined rotation, so that the mayordomía passes on to the next house or to the whole next block, in which case there is a whole group of mayordomos. In Tepetlaoxtoc, as in some of the other villages in the region, the mayordomo must find his own replacement; if he does not, he must repeat the cargo the following year. Below I discuss further the whole long-term process of ensuring a successor. Here, I am interested in the interaction that occurs between the mayordomo and his potential successor. Others have described similar interactions in other communities in passing but without attributing to them much significance (e.g., Hill and Monaghan 1987:18; Slade 1992:106, 112). In contrast, I wish to suggest that they are highly relevant to local understandings of personhood and action.

In Tepetlaoxtoc, the mayordomo must convince or coax his potential successor to accept the cargo, and the latter will always begin by refusing. He will do so even though at some time in the past he has let it be known that he wants to be mayordomo or has at least expressed some interest. The current mayordomo knows that the potential successor has expressed interest, which is why he is trying to convince this particular person. In the neighboring village of Chiconcuac, Dula Celina Rodríguez Hernández (2008) describes something similar. She finds that it is not considered correct to ask for a mayordomía, since this would be considered *soberbio* (arrogant). A person who wants to be mayordomo must go about it indirectly, by asking someone else to suggest to the current mayordomo *que lo tome en cuenta* (that he takes him into account) (2008:61).[5]

In Tepetlaoxtoc, after the mayordomo has identified someone who has expressed interest, he will likely go about this by plying his target with drink. He may go to the potential successor's house with a bottle specifically for this purpose or may take advantage of finding him at another fiesta. If the mayordomo finds his potential successor at another fiesta where there is music, he will pay the band to play songs especially for the potential successor. This convincing will not necessarily work, since it is possible that the potential successor really has decided to do the mayordomía at some point but does not feel ready to do it at this time, because he has not yet saved enough money and prepared his team. (Expressing interest in doing the mayordomía and then *never* doing it can get one in trouble with the saint, a point I return to below when I discuss the obligatory and voluntary nature of these actions.) However, if the potential successor is truly ready to be coaxed, his refusal will change to reluctance. He will start to say that he wants to do it but that he needs more compañeros.

Ignacio,[6] a fifty-year-old resident who fattens cattle for a living, told me about his recent experience passing a mayordomía to Agustín, a fellow villager of about the same age. He explained that before Agustín accepted the mayordomía from him, Agustín asked what he could offer, and Ignacio responded that he would offer Agustín fifteen compañeros including himself. The next week, Ignacio accompanied Agustín to the houses of all the other fourteen, whom Ignacio had already asked, and then after hearing their confirmations Agustín accepted the mayordomía. Note that although they had already told Ignacio they would do it, it was still necessary for Agustín to do the work of going to their homes and coaxing them to obtain their confirmation. If the current mayordomo did a poor job of recruiting compañeros—which is also achieved by coaxing their participation—he may have a hard time finding a successor because the potential successor

Figure 3.1 The Band of the González from the neighboring village of San Pedro Chiautzingo, performing during the fiesta of San Sebastián in Tepetlaoxtoc, January 2012. Photograph by Jaime Sanromán Ruiz.

knows that the mayordomo will not be able to offer him much help in the way of compañeros.

Because of the "work" and insecurity involved, finding a replacement is considered to be one of the more stressful aspects of being mayordomo. Even if one has laid the necessary groundwork through past efforts, there is no guarantee of finding a replacement and most do not have the time, money, or energy to want to do the mayordomía a second year in row. Agustín, for example, was unable to find a replacement and had to do the mayordomía a second time. Most people explained this failure in terms of the fact that he had not formed a good team and gotten others involved, which in turn they saw as a result of his attitude of superiority.

It is interesting that even though a potential successor may have dragged on his reluctance for weeks before accepting, the moment he does so, he leaves all signs of hesitation behind, displaying an energetic attitude of interest and dedication, described in local terms as "gusto." This shift in attitude does not mean, however, that he must deny his initial hesitation. When I asked people why they had taken on a mayordomía, they usu-ally recounted a similar narrative of not wanting to do it and then being

Figure 3.2 The dance of the "negritos" during the fiesta of San Sebastián in Tepetlaoxtoc, January 2012. Originally performed in Gulf Coast communities, this dance represents and honors the work of African slaves. Like other forms of participation in the fiesta, the dance must be performed with "buena gana" to avoid provoking the saint's wrath. Photograph by Jaime Sanromán Ruiz.

convinced by someone else, usually the previous mayordomo. What matters is that once a mayordomo accepts, all doubt must remain in the past.

This shift in attitude was particularly notable when I observed as a new *encargado* of a fireworks display for the first day of San Sebastián's fiesta accepted the post. I refer to the person in charge of this cargo as an *encargado* because the position does not have the official church designation of *mayordomía*. Thirty years ago a group of brothers and cousins decided to get together and sponsor a fireworks display for San Sebastián to signal the arrival of a pilgrimage from the neighboring village of San Pedro Chiautzingo on the first day of the eight-day-long celebration. Every year the group grew in size to include more extended family members and, more recently, friends and neighbors. With this growth in numbers, the total of the cooperaciones also increased and the fireworks display had also gotten longer and more elaborate. The practice worked like a mayordomía with an encargado who takes up collections of cooperaciones with the help of a few compañeros, and must find his replacement for the following year. The practice is a sort of proto-mayordomía. On this occasion, I had just observed from close-up as about twenty men set off over a thousand rockets and "bombs" of different types during about thirty minutes. I felt that I was in the middle of some sort of battle reenactment, as I coughed on the smoke and attempted to dodge sparks and falling rocket remains. Afterwards, the men brought out bottles, and we were serving each other mixes of cheap tequila and soft drinks and talking about how the display compared to the previous year's. At one point everyone gathered together; when I asked why, someone explained that they were choosing next year's replacement. There was, however, no election or a discussion over who should do it. Somehow they had already chosen their man, and although the current encargado was leading the way, the whole group was convincing or, more precisely, pushing him to do it. He refused, not seeming to take them seriously at first, but when they continued to push him he said that he could not do it because he had only been part of the group for a couple of years and he did not know how it worked. A few people said that he should not worry since everyone would help, and others argued that it was easy; one said specifically that it was easy because "the list was already there," referring to the list of people who participated that year and could be expected to do so again with the necessary "work" of collecting.

Eventually he accepted, and I noted that his attitude and bodily comportment changed immediately. Whereas while they were convincing him he seemed to shrink away from the group almost trying to cover or protect himself, after accepting he stood tall, stuck his chest out, and took on the bearing of a leader. Before they knew what was happening, he announced that three of the men who had been berating him most adamantly would be his compañeros. They looked surprised and not particularly pleased but were unable to protest after having just offered their help. A few moments later, he had produced a pad of paper and a pen and was going around gathering commitments for the following year; he soon convinced me to add my name to the list. His bodily comportment showed the attitude of "gusto" that one is supposed to feel in such a post. This change in attitude exemplifies why I refer to what villagers produce in each other as active *subjectivity*: what matters is not simply the action, but the subjective state or attitude with which it is performed.

Having a negative attitude about doing a religious cargo is, in fact, dangerous, because one can incur the wrath of the saint (see below). Yet there is another reason why this quick change in attitude is not really surprising: no one can *make* someone else do a religious cargo. There is no authority

Figure 3.3 Castillo (castle) of fireworks at the fiesta of San Sebastián in Tepetla-oxtoc, January 2012. The size and design of the castillo are important measures of the "participation" that the mayordomo has motivated in others. Photograph by Jaime Sanromán Ruiz.

that controls the actions of others in this context. It is not that villagers cannot imagine being controlled in this manner: they are familiar with it in wage-labor jobs, for example. Rather, action in the context of the fiestas is like that described by Marilyn Strathern (1988) for a gift economy: one's actions are inalienable; they can only be one's own. Again following Strathern's logic, while watching the scene of twenty men convincing and pushing the potential encargado, it is easy for a modern Western observer to think that they are trying to control his actions and that if he accedes he will be doing their bidding and his actions will really be theirs. However, in this context in the village, the agent and the actor are supposed to be separate and the relationship between people and their actions are not thought of in terms of "commodity economy" metaphors of ownership (Strathern 1988). People's actions are supposed to be produced by others. But this does not mean that the agent controls the actor; once someone begins to act, the action is all his own. He is doing it because he wants to, and so he does it as a subject or, in local terms, con gusto.

Doing the Fiesta Incorrectly: The Arrogance of Being Individualistic

Frequently, villagers explained to me what it means for the fiesta to be done "entre todos" through a contrast with the incorrect way of doing a fiesta, which interestingly sounds very much like the way anthropologists usually describe cargos. But it is important to note that the people who do it incorrectly according to Tepetlaoxtoc's residents are not the indigenous people usually described by anthropologists but instead urbanites more like the anthropologists themselves. Doing the fiesta incorrectly basically means doing it on one's own or, more precisely, thinking that one can do it on one's own: that is, that you can use your own money to sponsor the fiesta and all of its activities. One reason why this does not work is simply that it is too expensive for most villagers to do this. There is the cost of a comida, which the mayordomo has to cover, and then all of the fireworks, music, and other expenses for the day of the fiesta, which can amount to between fifty thousand and three hundred thousand pesos. In addition, there is the cost of the public work, usually in or around the church, that the mayordomía is supposed to contribute.

It is conceivable, however, that someone could have the necessary cash to do the fiesta. Yet if someone were to do a fiesta in this manner, people would not consider that it had been done well, and no one, or very few people, would show up to the meals or to the more public celebratory events such as the fireworks.[7] What makes it a poorly done fiesta is that instead of getting others involved, the mayordomo tried to do it on his own. I would even add that it is not simply that the mayordomo has done it poorly. Rather, he has missed the point of the fiesta entirely. People who try to do a fiesta on their own are described as being *presumidos* (braggarts or conceited), *altaneros* (feeling themselves above others), or *individualistas* (individualistic people). All three of these terms imply that they think that they do not need others—that they can do things on their own. Plus, there is an implication of foolishness since this is not "a different way of doing things"; rather, it is simply untrue that one does not need others. People who try to act on their own in such a manner are criticized for this—even as they are pitied for their foolishness—and others will tend to keep their distance, because no one wants to get involved in a failed mayordomía.

When Agustín accepted the mayordomía of the Santísima Trinidad (Holy Trinity) from Ignacio, he ended up doing what many people thought was a poor job. Agustín had spent his youth in the village and had then moved to Mexico City, where he worked as a *comerciante* (merchant),

Figure 3.4 The *torito* (little bull) is a fireworks display that interacts playfully with spectators; this one was photographed during the fiesta of San Sebastián, Tepetlaoxtoc, January 2012. Fireworks displays are costly and potentially dangerous, but villagers insist that they are necessary to make a fiesta beautiful, an opinion shared by the saints. Photograph by Jaime Sanromán Ruiz.

grinding and selling coffee, and then bought a truck and worked as a mover. He had tired of the crime in the city about eight years earlier and had returned to the village, where he has been working as an *albañil* (construction worker) ever since. When I asked him why he had taken on the mayordomía, he answered that he wanted to do something for the community, that his daughter-in-law and his granddaughter were both sick and wanted to help them, and that he thought everyone should be mayordomo at least once in his life and he had never done it before. His answers were different from those of most people and suggested a different understanding. In particular, hardly anyone talks about "doing something for the community," and Agustín omitted the seeming contradiction (see below) that people usually emphasize when they talk about taking on the mayordomía, which is that they do it out of an obligation to the saint and that they do it *por gusto* (that is, because they want to). After the fiesta, many people considered that Agustín had done a poor job because he had put on a small fireworks show and had included only a couple of entertainment activities in the fiesta's program, both implying that he had collected a small amount of money in cooperaciones. This, in turn, implied that he had gotten few people involved, including few compañeros, which was reflected in the low attendance at the fiesta's events. One villager explained to me that Agustín had had trouble because of his *grosero* (rude) or *presumido* (arrogant) attitude. He said that Agustín was already thought of as someone who felt he was superior to others and that he did not need others, and then the mayordomía made him feel like he was even more important, which turned people off further. Agustín himself seemed to be aware of this failure and it having something to do with how people saw him, but he blamed it on one of his compañeros spreading negative gossip about him.

This kind of individualistic behavior connected to doing the mayordomía incorrectly is not the same as the "selfishness" that we often associate with this category. It is not that they are keeping something for themselves or only thinking of themselves instead of the collective. In fact, they are potentially directing a significant amount of their resources to the fiesta and community, more than one would do as mayordomo if the fiesta were done the right way, by everyone. This kind of behavior is usually called "individualism" rather than "individualistic" in most modern, Western contexts and is seen in a positive light because it demonstrates independence and resolve as well as a preoccupation with the collective good. In contrast, villagers look critically upon such behavior because they consider it inappropriate that someone should think that he can act on his own. We might say that villagers are concerned with the way in which such actions are conducted and not with their ends (the celebration of the fiesta). But this is because the actions in themselves are also considered ends: what the mayordomo is supposed to produce is not simply the fiesta, nor the community, but rather other people's action or participation. And as we have seen, even the mayordomo's actions are a product of the previous mayordomo's provocation.

Participation through Inalienable Prestations

As I point out in the previous section, it is not really accurate to say that the mayordomo uses other people's money to put on the fiesta. Rather, he acts on the villagers' behalf, or they, in the form of the money they have cooperated with, act through him. This understanding of the role of cash in fiestas contrasts with social scientists' usual assumptions regarding the individualizing effects of money. Authors such as Georg Simmel and Karl Marx, when analyzing the emergence of modern capitalist society in Europe, described how commodification and the expanding uses of money enabled a separation between persons and things and between persons. These separations led to the emergence of the individualized person so important to modern Western society and thought. When conceptualizing the spread of modern Western culture to other parts of the world, we often assume that the process will occur in the same manner and that persons will necessarily be completely individualized by the spread of capitalism and commodification. This manner of thinking has been prevalent in analyses of Mesoamerican communities, primarily through the assumption that only by closing themselves off from global capitalism can communities survive at all as such (Cancian 1992; Wolf 1955). More specifically, it is often assumed that the introduction of cash into community activities is equivalent to their displacement by the market economy and the emergence of individualized persons. Jeffrey Cohen, for example, posits that when the Oaxacan villagers he studied starting paying others to do their communal labor (*tequio*), they were replacing "the social contract that tequio establishes between a Santañero household and the community" with "a business contract between an employer and employee" (1999:118). He also categorizes cooperaciones in cash for community projects and fiestas as a "tax." Yet Cohen does a superb job of including in his study the contrasts between villagers' understanding and his own, so that he also notes that villagers see the cooperaciones not as taxation—in the sense of something imposed from above—but as "monetary tequio" (1999:119). I would add that when these villagers pay others to do their communal labor, this is another form of "monetary tequio," since the business contract exists alongside of community relations and does not replace them. We could say that cash and the fluidity it provides allow communal labor to continue to exist in a modified form even in situations where people do not have the time to do the work themselves.

In Tepetlaoxtoc, villagers have replaced many activities with cash donations. Unlike more-isolated villages in other parts of Mesoamerica where cooperation for fiestas is expected either in the form of work, such as making tortillas at the mayordomo's house, or in kind, such as bringing tortillas (see Monaghan 1990), in Tepetlaoxtoc, it is understood that most people will cooperate by giving cash. This replacement of cash for work or for other kinds of things certainly allows for a kind of freedom in the sense that Simmel (1978 [1907]) saw in money. That is, it frees people from obligations to do a particular sort of work at a particular time, for example, making tortillas to bring to a fiesta or in an even more restricted sense, making tortillas at the mayordomo's house. This freedom is important to people in Tepetlaoxtoc because their time is restricted by the requirements of wage labor. In addition, cash has other advantages. Many of them have decent-paying wage-labor jobs, which means that the pay from an hour's work on the job can buy a lot more tortillas, for example, than they could produce themselves in an hour. Furthermore, most of the objects that villagers now consider necessary to put on a fiesta, such as fireworks, a musical band, and bottled alcoholic beverages, are not produced in the village and involve major expenditures that require the pooling of cash.

Thus, in Tepetlaoxtoc, cash may replace certain things such as work and tortillas, but my point here is that it cannot replace people. More concretely, money may separate persons from their bodily participation in *faenas* and fiestas, but a mayordomo cannot use his own cash to put on the fiesta by himself. Cash does not allow persons to act independently of others, as the modern individualized person is usually imagined to do (Strathern 1988). Being mayordomo *means* collecting cooperaciones in cash from others, getting them to participate. The mayordomo does not put on the fiesta himself using other people's money. Rather, it is through their cooperaciones that villagers participate in the fiesta, so that it can be said that "la fiesta se hace entre todos." People may say that the mayordomo did a good job, but they will quickly add, "Lo hicieron todos" ("Everyone did it"), since the mayordomo does not subsume others' participation—he acts on their behalf. Mayordomos themselves like to point out what has been accomplished, but they must be careful to acknowledge everybody's participation. They will also point out to people who participated what their money has done and bought, thus showing them that he has not forgotten their action or tried to claim it for himself. When they fail to acknowledge others' participation, criticism emerges. For example, when one villager took me to see his barrio's church, he saw me reading a plaque attached to the top of the entranceway to the church's property. It had the name of a mayordomo, those of his first three compañeros, and the year it was constructed, implying that this mayordomía had constructed the wall around the church and the gate as their project for the church. He scoffed at the plaque and said that they were going to remove it because the wall had been constructed "entre todos." I think that the cooperaciones people give to the mayordomo should be understood as a type of inalienable prestation.

Figure 3.5 The construction of an annex to the chapel of the Holy Trinity, financed by the "cooperations" collected by the mayordomía of the Holy Trinity. Tepetlaoxtoc, 2011.

In cooperating, people are detaching a part of themselves, and through this part they participate in the putting on of the fiesta.

Villagers talk about being present at the fiesta or accompanying the mayordomo, referring not necessarily to their bodily presence but rather to their cooperaciones. Even though villagers do not have a term to refer to this part of themselves that is contained in the products—in this case, cash—of their work, I believe that they are referring to what Good Eshelman's Nahua informants call *"fuerza"* or *"chicahualiztli"* (2004a:137). According to Good Eshelman, as people pass on their work (*tequitl*) to others, the latter also receive the former's fuerza, which has a generative capacity, making, in turn, the recipients' work productive (2004a:137). Similarly, in Tepetlaoxtoc, people's presence in their cooperaciones causes or motivates the mayordomo to work. Their presence in the cooperaciones is also what constitutes their togetherness when they put on the fiesta "entre todos," referring even to villagers who live elsewhere and do not physically attend the fiesta but have participated through a cooperación. Once again,

Good Eshelman's findings are germane: "Everyone, each in their own way, is incorporated into the unit through 'work'; it must be noted that internal heterogeneity is implicit and is necessary to their conception of unity" (2004a:137; my translation).

"El mismo dinero corre y corre"

Another common statement in relation to fiestas is "El mismo dinero corre y corre" ("The same money goes around and around"), usually accompanied by a circular motion of the hand. Alternatively, people may say, "Todo es solo prestado" ("Everything is only lent"). Briefly put, these statements refer to the fact that when a person gives money to a mayordomo, later on when that person takes on a mayordomía, the former mayordomo will give him a cooperación of the same amount of money. The idea and the actions represented by this statement are, however, not important in the same way that la fiesta se hace entre todos is important. The latter is the point of it all, while the former is just something that occurs or should be made to occur while the latter gets done. The existence of this kind of reciprocal exchange means that the fiesta or the mayordomía cannot be understood as isolated occurrences but rather as a chain of events, as others have noted (Brandes 1988; Cohen 1999; Monaghan 1990). John Monaghan, in an effort to counter anthropologists' tendency to speak of this kind of exchange in the technical language of redistribution, notes that in Nuyoo, Oaxaca, these prestations are talked about "in terms of mutual aid and not in the accountant[-]like language of credits and debts, despite the precise records they keep" (1990). I understand Monaghan as saying that even if people expect to get back what they gave, what they emphasize is helping others do the fiesta and not the "loan" aspect of this help.

In Tepetlaoxtoc, hearing accountant-like language is likewise uncommon. And again, while people do need financial help to put on the costly fiestas, this mutual aid aspect of the cooperaciones is not what matters most about them. It could be said that in Tepetlaoxtoc what matters most is that the exchange occurs at all. The passing of money from one hand to another is how people participate and how the fiesta is put on "among everyone." While the value of the cash given is necessary so that the mayordomo can buy things for the fiesta, the fact that the cash was given in the first place is necessary to him in the sense of allowing him to do his job of getting others involved, of producing them as active subjects. Meanwhile, the mayordomo is also helping the donor, who needs the mayordomo's coaxing to allow him to participate. The donor also needs this transaction to occur for another reason: it will later allow him to be mayordomo and to coax the current mayordomo into participation. Perhaps I have already made my point, but I could still add that the donor also helps the current mayordomo by setting up a situation that will allow the latter to be a donor and thus a participant in the future. In this sense, people's actions anticipate future action, and they do so through another person (see Regehr 2005). Other anthropologists have described something similar, but in terms of the resources needed to put on the fiesta. Knowing that he will be mayordomo in the future, a person will try to accumulate credits, and this money will allow him to do the fiesta when he is mayordomo. In Tepetlaoxtoc, I would say that someone who wants to do a mayordomía in the future is not accumulating only monetary credits but also potential for action, stored in other persons. Another way of thinking of these transactions involves recalling that the cooperaciones are parts of their donors. And thus it is the people, in the form of their money, who "go around and around" from one fiesta to another, inciting each other to act.

A mayordomo who considers cooperaciones to be like a personal favor or a loan will receive criticism. When Agustín was mayordomo, I attended the comida he gave for the fiesta, and I was a bit surprised when he personally gave me a bottle of tequila apart from the bottle that was placed on the table for people to consume during the meal. At first I was confused by his action and guessed that he was giving me the bottle to serve people at the table. But when I asked someone sitting nearby, he said that Agustín had given it to me, and I could do what I wanted with it, even suggesting that I take it home unopened. When I mentioned this to Ignacio on another occasion, he said that Agustín had probably done this because of the five hundred pesos I had given him as a cooperación. He added, however, that this was somewhat inappropriate because the meal, which the mayordomo pays for with his own money, is separate from the cooperaciones, implying that Agustín should have waited and returned my money to me only if I were to become mayordomo. My cooperación was never possessed by him in a way that it could be paid back. He could return the favor, but only through participating if I were to become mayordomo and not by returning my money in another manner.

Putting together "un equipo" to do the mayordomía also involves action over the long term. It involves setting things, or more accurately, other people in motion years before. One forty-year-old informant, Antonio, was always very interested in talking about the fiesta de la Santísima and the mayordomía. I asked him if he himself wanted to be mayordomo, and he said yes, in a few years. When I asked whether he was waiting in order to save money, he answered that he needed time to "formar un equipo." Over the next couple of years, I observed as Antonio served as a compañero in the mayordomía, standing out (in the eyes of other villagers and in particular the mayordomo) among the other compañeros for his diligence. Others explained his dedication in terms of his great devotion to the saint;[8] while I do not doubt this, I also think that it was clear to Antonio that he was setting things in motion to put together his team for a future mayordomía. It would be more accurate to say that he let himself be put into motion by the mayordomos whom he helped as compañero. Later on, he would set these mayordomos in motion as compañeros for his own mayordomía. To give a contrasting example, when Alfonso, a sixty-year-old construction contractor, took on the St. Vicente mayordomía as a sort of emergency measure after it had been completely abandoned the year before, he complained that it was going to be very difficult for him to put together a team. The motion from the past had come to a halt, and without this momentum Alfonso had the difficult task of starting from a standstill. In the example of Antonio, although some members of his team had been mayordomos in previous years, others were waiting for Antonio to set them in motion, enabling them to take on a mayordomía in the future. This is why forming a good, large, and dedicated team is necessary not only for doing the fiesta but for finding a replacement as well: these future mayordomos are potential replacements. (Recall that people explained Agustín's failure to find a replacement by the fact that he had not put together *un buen equipo*, "a good team.")

Why People Put on the Fiesta: Gusto and Obligación

When people talk about why they participate in the fiestas and mayordomías, it is not uncommon to hear what seemed to me, at least at first, as a blatant contradiction. In one sentence people would say that participation is *voluntaria* (voluntary) or *por gusto* (for pleasure) and then soon after, sometimes in the very next sentence, they would say that it is *obligatoria* (obligatory) or *algo que tienen que hacer* (something that they have to do). People also spoke of civil cargos in a similar manner. On one occasion, I asked the president of the Comité de Bienes Comunales (Committee for Communal Property) how he had ended up with the cargo. He explained that he had won the most votes in a village assembly and that the villagers *"Me comprometieron"* ("They committed me"). However, a couple of sentences later, he emphasized the fact that he had volunteered for the post before the election. At moments, or perhaps just for my benefit, villagers themselves seemed to see the ridiculousness of describing their motivation in this manner. Once, an informant was telling me that participation was voluntary, but then he started to laugh and added that really you had to do it. However, in practice, as I will now try to show, there is no contradiction, and participation, in fact, *must* be both voluntary and obligatory.

Most anthropologists working in contemporary Mesoamerica have avoided this apparent contradiction by turning it into a debate among themselves as to whether fiestas and mayordomías are more about social service and community solidarity or about individual access to prestige. Jeffrey Cohen is an exception in that he notes that for his informants, cargos are about altruism and self-interest at the same time (1999:123). It is important to take Cohen's observation a step further and try to understand how and why it would make sense for someone to label something both voluntary and obligatory in two consecutive sentences. The conundrum is obviously not new to anthropology, although most Mesoamericanists have managed to sidestep this important anthropological debate. Marcel Mauss (1990 [1923]) and Bronislaw Malinowski (1926) pondered over similar apparent contradictions in the latter's data on Trobriand gift exchange, sometimes falling into the old individual-society dichotomies and at other times grasping that something quite distinct was going on and that perhaps for the Trobrianders something could be voluntary and obligatory at the same time.[9] Since then, authors such as Roy Wagner (1981 [1975]) and Marilyn Strathern (1988) have helped us to imagine how this could be in the Melanesian case and beyond by revealing the pitfalls of imposing on our informants our own notions of the person and action.

In Tepetlaoxtoc, many people talk about their motivation for participation in terms of the saints, often in the form of stories about themselves or about other villagers. Most of these stories concern the patron saint of the whole village, San Sebastián, who is often simply referred to as "*el patrón*." This would translate directly as "the patron," but I think they use it more in the sense of "the chief" or "the boss," and San Sebastián often seems to rank even above Jesus and the Virgin Mary in the supernatural religious hierarchy. Villagers state that San Sebastián is "*muy milagroso, pero muy castigador*" ("very miraculous, but very punishing"), and most of their stories about the saint and participation have to do with his punishing villagers or the threat of his doing so. For example, Francisco, a sixty-five-year-old villager, told me that one year his father was a compañero for one of the mayordomías of San Sebastián and so Francisco's mother needed chickens to prepare a meal. Francisco's father had seventy chickens and told Francisco's mother to take what she needed. She took only a few, however, and some days later the rest of the chickens died without any apparent explanation, although Francisco believed that it was a lesson from San Sebastián telling them not to be so cheap. Francisco also recounted that he usually gives a thousand pesos to one of the mayordomías for San Sebastián, but one year he told the mayordomo when he came to collect the cooperación that he would give him five hundred before the fiesta and another five hundred after, but only if he burned enough fireworks. Just as he finished saying this, *un cohete* (a rocket)[10] exploded just beside his gas tanks. He took this as a message from the saint and quickly ran inside for another five hundred pesos to give to the mayordomo. From these stories, it seems obvious that the saint obliges people to participate.

Another kind of story demonstrates the necessity of participation being voluntary. Almost everyone can tell stories of people who were punished by San Sebastián for participating *con mala gana* or *sin buena gana*, which basically means to do something with a poor attitude — it is the opposite of doing something *con gusto*. One common story is of a person who agreed to dance for San Sebastián during a fiesta but did it with mala gana and fell off the stage and broke his leg. Another tells of a man who was carrying a bundle of *cohetes* during a procession for San Sebastián, but with mala gana. He lit a rocket, and it shot straight up in the air, came back down, and exploded in his bundle, setting off the other rockets and blowing the man to pieces. So San Sebastián obligates people to participate, but participation in itself is not enough. The saint will also punish them unless they participate con gusto, that is, unless they participate willingly and with a positive attitude that demonstrates this willingness.

The voluntary nature of participation matters not just to the saint but to mortals as well. In fact, it seems that forced participation really is not participation at all, and that no participation may even be better than forced participation. In Tepetlaoxtoc, I did not hear of either mayordomos or civil cargo holders forcing participation. However, in some neighboring villages they do in extreme cases where people continue to refuse to participate in mayordomos or faenas. The civil authorities may attempt to force participation by cutting off people's water supply or even putting them in jail (see Encarnación Ruiz 2004; Ennis-McMillan 2001). However, the cargo holders seem to want to avoid this measure as long as possible because what they really want is to convince the person to participate "voluntarily" and not to force him to do so. Junior Encarnación Ruiz (2004) describes a case in the neighboring village of San Juan Tezontla in which a man who refused to participate in religious and civil community activities was eventually approached by the *delegados*, the highest-ranking civil authorities in the community. While the delegados had the authority to immediately coerce the man into participating by threatening to cut off his water supply or throw him in jail, they spent hours trying to convince him to participate, which they eventually achieved. Encarnación Ruiz notes that both the delegados and the man who originally refused to participate left the meeting looking genuinely relieved and content. The delegados were not happy simply because the villager was going to participate but because he was going to do so voluntarily, and the villager's contentment was not due to the fact that he had avoided jail time, but because he was going to join others in working for the community.

I think the saint's and the villagers' apparently contradictory expectations begin to make sense if we look at what people mean when they speak of something being obligatory or voluntary. I think that when villagers speak of "obligation" they mean this more in the sense of a commitment or fulfilling others' expectations than in the sense of a compulsion or requirement. Villagers see themselves as having such an obligation or commitment to the saint and to their fellow villagers or to "the community." When they say this they are referring to the fact that the fiesta is supposed to be done "entre todos" and that others thus expect them to do their part and participate. Once I met a man from a neighboring village, and as I turned the conversation to the topic of participation he said that his family had a tradition of making *tapetes* (woven mats) and hanging them in the church for *el día de la Virgen* (the day of the Virgin of Guadalupe). I asked him why they did it, and he said it was an obligation. When I asked what he meant by *obligation*, he answered that it was like *una ley* (a law). When I inquired as to what would happen if they did not do it, expecting some form of severe punishment after his reference to the law, he surprised me by saying, "The tradition would be lost." When I asked who the obligation was to, he answered that it was to the community, by which I understand that it was something the community expected of them and caused them to do but was not something anybody was requiring of them. I think that his reference to "una ley" was meant to convey the seriousness of the commitment to other villagers but really had nothing to do with compulsion or the potential for punishment. In other words, the commitment means that other people (such as the mayordomo and his compañeros) need one's help and participation. And when people talk about the obligatory nature of participation they are also referring to the fact that their actions are caused by others.

When people say that participation is voluntary, they are referring to the fact that villagers do it because they want to, not because they are forced. Recall that while the mayordomo causes others to act, he always does so by coaxing. This coaxing can be quite persistent but never takes on the tone of trying to force someone to act. During his coaxing, the mayordomo will focus neither on the obligatory aspect of the participation nor on past debts but rather on the positive or enjoyable aspects of the fiesta: the beauty of the music and the fireworks and the enjoyment of the *convivencia*. He will also remind the potential donor of the fact that they all need each other and of the beauty of doing the fiesta entre todos: all reasons not just for participating but for doing so con gusto. The very act of asking for the cooperación is putting this need for others into practice: the mayordomo is demonstrating that he needs the potential donor. The mayordomo needs the donor's cooperación to be able to do the fiesta entre todos, and the donor needs the mayordomo to convince him. Thus, participation is simultaneously obligatory and voluntary, since one participates to fulfill others' expectations or needs at the same time that this fulfillment of others' needs is considered one of life's great joys, something that gives life meaning, and thus something that one wants to do. The fact that such actions are both voluntary and obligatory is another way of saying that people cause each other to act but without controlling each other, or, to put this in still another way, that they produce active subjectivity in others.

Prestige versus Reconocimiento (Recognition)

I think that many of the anthropologists who have studied fiestas and cargo systems, at least since the publication of Cancian's now-classic work (1965), take for granted that mayordomos and other cargo holders gain some amount of prestige for holding cargos. As in many studies of gift exchange in other world regions, it is imagined that donors, or in the Mexican case, cargo holders, who distribute their wealth rank above recipients. The notion of prestige helps to translate this idea of rank into the more familiar idiom of accumulation. Thus we arrive at the comprehensible formula of the conversion of material accumulation into "symbolic" accumulation (prestige) by giving the former away or redistributing it. Prestige can then be converted into power, since it gives its owner a sort of moral authority over others. In the end, we imagine that these peoples who live in a world of gift exchange are different from us because they cannot control others directly through material wealth; in other words, they do not exercise power over others by buying their labor. Rather, they must first convert material wealth into prestige and then exercise power through a sort of moral debt. Therefore, while the two systems are different, they are also similar because they share the final objective of control over other people.

Recently, a few anthropologists working in the region have begun to question the notion that individual accumulation of prestige is what motivates participation in cargos. Catharine Good Eshelman, for example, argues that fiestas "[a]re not vehicles for individual indebtedness or impoverishment, nor do they create a hierarchy of prestige (Cancian 1965), because they mobilize resources through a reciprocal network and the Nahuas consider the expenditures to be collective rather than individual. I suggest that these circumstances are similar in many other places but that they have not been documented with sufficient care" (2004a:134; my translation). Doren Slade (1992:15) posits that a cargo holder motivated by self-interest is actually dangerous because self-interest threatens "core assumptions that hinge on balance and harmony necessary for social order." She continues: "I learned that men who had served collective aims well were considered *importante*, and notable for being steadfast in the performance of their duties. These men were also *recto*, righteous and just, and of good reputation, which earned them respect. In contrast, a demonstration of pride (*orgullo*) in one's accomplishments, especially those stemming from desire for self-enhancement, invited mistrust and was typically associated with prideful ambition" (1992:15–16). Monaghan (2008), meanwhile, suggests that people do not take on cargos for what they will receive in return, because they feel that they owe what they already have to the community. In contrast to the notion that the individual is prior to and responsible for the creation of the group, in Mesoamerica, the group is seen as prior to the individual and "wealth and good fortune one may enjoy is made possible by the fact that one lives in a community. Liturgies and cargos thus give one the opportunity to acknowledge this benefit and fulfill a kind of contract" (2008:26). I believe that all of these formulations could be applied to Tepetlaoxtoc. However, I will contribute here another understanding of the limitations of the prestige model that emerges through attention to local understandings of personhood and action and, in particular, to the local notion that the cargo holder produces something of value—action in others—but does not own and thus cannot accumulate this product and its value.

I began to feel suspicious of the application of the prestige model to Tepetlaoxtoc when I noticed that in relation to the mayordomías or other cargos, no one ever spoke of *prestigio* (prestige) but instead used the term

ser conocido (to be known) or *reconocimiento* (recognition). On one occasion, Lupita, a sixty-year-old woman who worked as a nurse in Mexico
City before retiring and returning to Tepetlaoxtoc, was trying to explain
to me why Agustín had had trouble getting people to participate when he
was mayordomo. She said that it was because Agustín *"no es conocido"*
("is not known"). Figuring that she meant this in the sense that people
did not know who he was, I asked if this was because he had lived outside
the village for a number of years. Identifying my confusion, she said that
everyone in the village knows everyone else in this sense, except perhaps
for children. She then clarified that when she said that "Agustín no es
conocido" she meant that people have not seen him *trabajando* (working)
in other fiestas or in faenas. I came to understand that she was saying that
he was not known for his participation. She was talking about what I might
think of as his reputation or lack thereof in relation to fiestas. She added
that whole families can be "known" as people who participate and *traba-
jan bien* (work correctly), so that people will readily give cooperaciones to
mayordomos from certain families even if the mayordomo himself is young
and not yet known.

One day I decided to mention to Ignacio the connection anthropologists
draw between cargos and prestige. When I finished, he asked me, "¿Quieres
decir 'reconocimiento'?" ("Do you mean 'recognition'?"), with a puzzled
look on his face. I answered that I was quite sure that the anthropologists
write about "prestige" and not "recognition." Without my prompting him,
he went on to explain that he did not think that prestige had anything to do
with why people participate. He said that people who already have prestige
take on mayordomías, so this would not be a reason for them to do so. He
did not seem to think very much of "prestige" in any case: he said that
prestige *"no dura mucho"* ("doesn't last long") and elaborated, "El prestigio
brilla pero es superfluo" ("Prestige is shiny but it's superfluous"). He noted
that the municipal presidents are often interested in prestige but that most
people in the village look down on this and would not want such men in
the really important cargos, such as the Comité de Agua Potable (Drinking
Water Committee) or the mayordomías, where the holder must be trusted
with the community's possessions.

He explained that the people who are elected for important civil cargos
"están reconocidos por su edad, su experiencia o su conocimiento" ("are
recognized for their age, their experience, or their knowledge"). More than
anything, they are people who are trusted because they have demonstrated
that they can be trusted through their past actions. Then, in an effort to
explain why people take on the cargos that are not decided by elections,

such as mayordomías, he insisted, "La participación es lo que importa" ("The participation is what matters") and added, "Conformo con que salgo y me saludan" ("For me it's enough if I go out and people greet me"). His formulation fits with the idea that the mayordomo gains nothing through his work since he is not making a sacrifice for the community—at least no more sacrifice than anyone else—because he is not the only one putting on the fiesta. In other terms, the mayordomo produces something valuable—others' participation—but this value belongs, in the end, not to him but to the actors themselves.

I believe that Ignacio was trying to help me to understand cargos, but he was also trying to distance himself from and to critique local politicians and petty capitalists who go against his ideals of equality and interdependence. These local elites remind villagers not only of the earlier exclusionary nature of village life but also of the manner in which politicians and employers in the city treat persons as objects. I can imagine that Cancian (1965) or others might claim that their own version of "prestige" is closer to Ignacio's concept of recognition than to his use of prestige, but in any case I find this locally formulated contrast illustrative of how villagers have reinvented or at least clarified their understanding of fiestas and cargos in opposition to hierarchies within the community and without. Villagers insist that what matters about fiestas are their fellow villagers and actions rather than any kind of *thing* such as prestige or power that an individual might accumulate.

People will often show pride in being conocidos, but that cannot be converted into what we would usually understand as power, at least not in the sense of control over other people. Recall that participation is voluntary and that no one controls anybody else in these contexts—ideally, not even those with "official" authority such as a *presidente* or a *delegado municipal*. It could be said that when the mayordomo convinces someone to participate, both parties win, albeit in different ways, but no one gains anything that can be converted into power or control over others. The mayordomo has performed his duty and produced value in the form of an active subject. However, this value also belongs to the actor himself, and he, rather than the mayordomo, takes the credit for his actions. If not, he would not be acting as a subject at all but rather as an object of the mayordomo's bidding.

I should note that although villagers tend to downplay hierarchy, the cargos and fiestas do produce distinctions among them, as suggested by the fact that some are more recognized or known for their participation than others. These distinctions hardly constitute a structured hierarchy, and it might be more accurate to describe them as distinctions of importance rather than prestige or power. That is, villagers who are known for their participation are important to the success of community practices such as fiestas because they can be relied on to participate and to spread their enthusiasm to others, causing in turn, their participation. If people who are conocido have anything like power, it is the power to get the wheel rolling and to get the fiesta celebrated "entre todos." However, the wheel metaphor has its limitations, because although a good mayordomo is needed by others, he also needs *them*, and thus it seems problematic to me to describe this position as one involving power. If anything, I would say that such people are important in the community, or they might be seen as "key" persons, to borrow a term from Minerva López Millán (2008; see chapter 4), in the sense that things might not happen or, more specifically, the fiesta would not get celebrated well without them. It might be even more useful to think of them as keystones, playing a special role in making the fiesta happen, yet in a manner that makes them fully dependent on the community's other members. They are important and in demand, but they are not powerful, in the sense that they do not have power over others nor do they control them.

Doing Things "Among Everyone" as a General Principle

I should note here that people in Tepetlaoxtoc see this notion of doing something *entre todos* (among everyone) as a manner in which life should be lived in general and not just as the correct way of doing fiestas. Along the same lines, my aim in this chapter is to describe the principle of doing something entre todos, using a description and analysis of mayordomías and fiestas as a means to this end and not as an end in itself. The generality of this principle can be seen, for example, in the fact that villagers sometimes complain that with the influence of the city, their children act individualistically and think that independence is admirable and other people are not essential. They try to teach their children that we all need others, stating this as a fact of life or human universal, not just as one of Tepetlaoxtoc's *tradiciones* (traditions). One of the basic ways that this principle is manifested in everyday life is the act of *saludando* (greeting) everyone that one passes on the street. Greeting everyone on the street demonstrates recognition of the fact that one is not alone in this world and needs others. In fact, something as apparently simple as greeting others on the street is seen as being closely tied to participation in fiestas. It was explained to me that those who do not greet others do not participate themselves and cannot get others to do so if they take on a mayordomía.

This principle is also present whenever villagers drink alcoholic beverages together: they never serve themselves. If one person is serving a group of people sitting at a table, he will pass the bottle to someone else rather than serve his own drink. If someone has finished his drink and wants more and no one offers he will pass the bottle to someone else asking to be served. When I asked people why they do this, they sometimes answered, "Un burro no se carga solo" ("A donkey doesn't load himself"). Another common response was to ask whether I would like to die alone or, alternatively, whether I would prefer to drink alone or with others.[11]

Funerals are another moment when the importance of doing things "entre todos" is apparent. Villagers say that at a funeral it is important that people other than one's own family members carry the casket. The presence of non-family members to carry the casket demonstrates that the deceased was *un buen vecino* (a good neighbor), which basically refers to someone who has always participated when called upon and has recognized his need of others. This last act of needing others (to carry the casket) and their willingness to do so indicate a life well-lived in this sense. In contrast, it is considered shameful if there is no one else willing to carry the casket and the deceased's own family members must do it.

When referring to most public works in the village such as roads, the water system, and schools, people say that they are *de todos* (everybody's) or say, "Se hizo entre todos" ("It was built by everybody").[12] They say this because these public works were built through *faenas*, a practice of collective labor in which all married male villagers are supposed to cooperate with either a day's work or a day's wage. The civil cargo holders—for example, *el presidente del* Comité de Agua Potable (the president of the Drinking Water Committee)—are supposed to organize faenas in the same way that mayordomos organize fiestas: by getting others to participate.

"Public" is in fact not an appropriate word for describing these works, since they are understood to belong not to the state or to the population in general but to "everyone," where *everyone* only refers to community members. Being a member of the community, in turn, is not a question of residence: living in the village or even being born in the village does not qualify someone for community membership. Community membership, rather, is determined first of all by descent from other community members and in some sense by participation. That is, someone from outside the village who participates over an extended period of time will be treated as a de facto community member even though villagers will remember that *no es de la comunidad* (he's not of the community). Even his children will be considered to be from elsewhere unless they are the offspring of a union with a community member. Meanwhile, a community member by descent who does not participate will be treated as an outsider even though everyone recognizes that he is of the community.

This separation between "public" and community is evident in local understandings of the village's water system. Although the office of the Comité de Agua Potable is housed in the municipal building, members of the community are careful to point out that the system *es del pueblo y no del municipio* (is the pueblo's and not the municipio's) because the people of the village built it and maintain it, not the municipal government. When they say that these works belong to the pueblo, they are referring not to a unit of the state or to a place but to the people who built the works or to their descendants. This particular notion of ownership is used to explain why people from outside the community who want water must pay as much as ten times more for the initial connection. The fact that these outsiders are Mexican citizens is irrelevant. They state that because these people did not cooperate in the building of the system, they must pay a different amount. They also see the village's churches and chapels in this same manner: they belong not to the Catholic Church but to the pueblo.[13] Once during a mass at the Holy Trinity Chapel, the parish priest was talking about how each family takes care of its house, and then he mentioned the chapel and asked, "¿De quién es la casa en este caso?" ("Whose house is it in this case?"). A chorus of voices answered, "De todos" ("Everyone's"). He seemed somewhat surprised at their answer and he asked again. When no one answered, he said, "De Dios" ("It's God's"), although obviously his congregation did not agree. Later, outside the church, a villager walked by and inquired if I needed anything. I responded by asking whether it was okay for me to serve myself from the two-liter bottle of soda on a nearby table. He nodded and added, not without irony, "Es la casa de todos" ("It's everybody's house").

FOUR

Ayuda Among and Within Families

The topic I treat in this chapter, that of family or kinship, is of interest to me because, as in the case of the community and the cargo system, it offers an opportunity to contrast our usual anthropological interest in the production of objects with a local interest in the production of active subjects. Family has not caught the attention of anthropologists working in Mesoamerica to the degree of cargo systems and community, but it has received considerable attention. Following disciplinary as well as broader modern Western cultural tendencies, anthropologists working in Meso-america have treated family as a site for biological and social reproduction, with, of course, a focus on those aspects of reproduction that people, as opposed to nature, are imagined to have some hand in. We could say that this includes the object-aspects of the person, as opposed to what we usu-ally understand as the subject-aspects such as personality or will, which usually fall beyond sociocultural anthropology's scope because they are seen as innate. So, for example, there is an interest in how peasants living under difficult circumstances manage to reproduce their bodies or "sur-vive" through food production, distribution, and ingestion and through care during illness. Also, in a manner similar to studies of community, we have shown a frequent interest in the local production of social systems, units, and structures or, more specifically, in the reproduction of the family or kinship units into the next generation.

In contrast to these interests in the production or reproduction of objects at the levels of the person and the social, it is assumed that nature, and not the family members as subjects, takes care of the production of the subject-aspects of the person. That is, persons are naturally endowed with the desire and ability to act. My objective here is to question this formulation and to suggest that while the production of object-aspects of persons does occur in families, it does so alongside of or perhaps even as a by-product of the *social* production of active subjects by family members. Further, I suggest that the fact that this production occurs in families has nothing to do with the notion of family being close to nature or to its supposed role as mediator between nature and culture (Schneider 1984). When I talk about the production of active subjects, I am not referring to parents instilling subjectivity in their children, for the first and only time, to then send them out into the world. Rather, for both parents *and* children the family is a site for a continuous production of active subjectivity in each other.

While I will not attempt a review of the extensive and varied literature on family in Mesoamerica (but see Mulhare 2000; Regehr 2005; Robichaux 2005b), I would like to provide a couple of examples of this treatment of the family as a site for the production and reproduction of objects or object-aspects of the person. First, a treatment of the family as a site for the reproduction of object-aspects of the person can be seen quite clearly in a genre of studies, mostly conducted by Mexican anthropologists, that focus on the manner in which the peasant family manages to survive and reproduce itself from its subordinate position in the broader capitalist economy (e.g., Arizpe 1980; Bartra 1978; Durand 1983; Lomnitz 1977; Palerm 1980; Warman 1980). Lourdes Arizpe, for example, makes her relation to these assumptions quite clear: "In this work, the countryside-city migration will be analyzed from the perspective of the dynamic of the composition of the peasant economy, as a strategy of the peasant families to survive and to reproduce themselves in the face of economic pressure from the industrial capitalist sector" (1980; my translation). Simply put, the peasant family is a social unit dedicated to the reproduction and survival of its members, or at least their object-aspects.

Another tendency, particularly prominent among American anthropologists, has been to take a traditional anthropological approach to kinship, treating it in terms of system and structure. In these studies, attention is given to the form that kinship relations take, the subtleties of how family and other kinship units are defined, and the relationship among the development of the domestic cycle, patterns of residency, and rules of inheritance (e.g., Nutini 1968; Nutini, Carrasco, and Taggart 1976; Sandstrom 1991; Taggart 1991 [1975]). Hugo Nutini's call for further study of the following three topics in Mesoamerican kinship is representative of this tendency: "(1) the study of comparative kinship *systems* in depth; (2) the study of kinship through the combination of synchronic and diachronic dimensions; (3) the formulation of a cognatic or bilateral theory of kinship" (1976:20; my emphasis). I should note that when Nutini mentions diachrony and a "cognatic or bilateral theory" he is referring to different approaches to what remains his main interest: kinship as system (1976). This concern with systems recalls the interest in cargos discussed above, once again focusing our analyses on how people create organization and structure in their lives. My point here is not that these systems and structures are insignificant but that they are interesting to us, with our focus on the production of things, in a manner that they are not as important to our informants, with their interest in producing active subjects.

In recent years, in the place of the studies that viewed families as economic survival units, there have been important advances toward adding questions of conflict and power to our understandings of families (e.g., González de la Rocha 1994; Rothstein 1982; Stephen 1991). Meanwhile, others have taken significant steps to increase our sophistication in our approach to local forms of kinship and family organization (e.g., Monaghan 1995; Robichaux 1997, 2005a, 2005c, 2008). But these new approaches to the Mesoamerican family still do not deal with important critiques (e.g., Schneider 1984; Yanagisako 1979) from the discipline in general aimed at the "folk" origins of our theoretical assumptions about what family and kinships are about. In consequence, a basic assumption about the family as a site of reproduction of the object-aspects of persons and of kinship systems remains and will continue to do so until we make these assumptions explicit and are able to look beyond them in our ethnography. Once again, my objective here is not to deny that the production of object-aspects of persons occurs in families but to suggest a shift in focus to highland Mexican people's interest in the production of active subjects in the context of the family, something usually attributed to nature. A few authors have begun this task (see Good Eshelman 2004b, 2005; López Millán 2008; Magazine and Ramírez Sánchez 2007; Ramírez Sánchez 2003; Regehr 2005; Taggart 2007).

My goal in this chapter is to contribute to this effort by demonstrating how many of family members' actions are directed toward producing action in other persons, either in different families or in their own. This kind of action generally takes the form of prestations or exchanges of what is referred to in the Texcoco region as *ayuda* (help). At the interfamily level, exchanges among different family groups, usually interpreted by anthropologists as mutual aid and as being about the things exchanged or about the production of relationships (e.g., Cohen 1999; Lomnitz 1977;

Stephen 1991), should also be understood as efforts to produce action in other families and a literal togetherness created as persons pass an inalienable part of themselves to others in these exchanges of labor and goods (see Good Eshelman 2004a, 2005).

At the intrafamily level, these exchanges occur primarily between generations, as parents act to cause their children to act and vice versa. Briefly put, parents provide ayuda to their children in the form of nurturance when the latter are young and then inheritance when they are older and marry. Sons and daughters, meanwhile, provide ayuda to their parents by contributing their labor or their earnings to the family economy and then, later on, by caring for their parents in old age. Of course, these exchanges achieve the reproduction of the person-as-object, but they are, I think, no more reducible to this function than are cargos to the reproduction of community structure and to the putting on of fiestas. More importantly, these prestations *constitute* being a son, daughter, mother, or father, and they produce the corresponding subjectivity in the recipient.[1] Further, these exchanges of ayuda constitute a particular kind of togetherness among family members that does not necessarily imply their sharing of objectives or acting as a family "unit."

At both the inter- and intrafamily levels, the practices surrounding the exchange of ayuda are analogous to the *participación* and *cooperación* at the community level described in the previous chapter. The term *ayudar* in Spanish generally means "to help" or "to aid." However, in the case of Tepetlaoxtoc and similar villages, I think that this translation probably causes us more confusion than good. Just as *cooperar* is not simply about helping the mayordomo pay for something he cannot afford himself, *ayuda* is not just about helping others out through material exchanges: it is also about needing others to be able to act or, in other words, about the problem of creating active subjects.[2] In this sense, we should view the material objects and labor that people exchange as a means to an end more than an end in themselves.

While the use of a Nahuatl term such as *palehuia* (Regehr 2005) instead of *ayuda* might create distance from our usual understanding of "help" and encourage us to remember that we are talking about something different even if the word is familiar, I have decided not to do so for two reasons: first, because in most of the villages in the Texcoco region, including Tepetlaoxtoc, they no longer use or even know the Nahuatl term; and second, because *palehuia* and other Nahuatl terms are awkward and hard to remember and pronounce for non-Nahuatl speakers such as myself and, I imagine, most of my readers.

Interfamily Ayuda

Briefly put, *interfamily ayuda* in Tepetlaoxtoc and other villages in the region refers to prestations given from one married couple or one nuclear family to another. This occurs most frequently when the receiving family is putting on a fiesta for a life-cycle ritual for one of its sons or daughters, such as a baptism, fifteenth birthday party (for girls), or wedding. In such cases, ayuda can be provided in the form of labor, as when women help other women to prepare the food for the fiesta, or in the form of objects such as animals, crops, money, and bought items including beverages, food, and disposable cups and plates (López Millán 2008:143). Similar prestations in the form of labor and objects are also made from one family to another whose members are providing a meal as part of a mayordomía. These donations are distinguished from the cooperaciones given to the mayordomo for the fiesta itself, to pay for the fireworks and music in communal spaces such as plazas, since the meal is supposed be something that the mayordomo, or one of his compañeros, pays for himself as opposed to paying for it with the cooperaciones. In addition, *ayuda* is sometimes used to refer to the aid one nuclear family receives from another for family projects such as harvesting crops or building a house. In Tepetlaoxtoc, for example, many families do not have to hire *albañiles* (construction workers) when they build a house, because almost everyone has a brother, cousin, *compadre* (co-godparent), or close friend who is *un albañil* and is willing to "help" through his own labor and by guiding the male members of the family doing the building.

Anthropologists have paid little attention to interfamily ayuda in rural Mesoamerica, probably because of the distraction created by the civil-religious hierarchy, which seduced us in its appearance as the community's social structure. I must admit that I also neglected this topic to an extent in my own research, which is why I rely heavily on other authors' work in this chapter, in particular that of Minerva López Millán (2008) in the village of Santa Catarina del Monte, located in Texcoco's sierra. Perhaps because of the absence of a civil-religious hierarchy, anthropologists working among rural migrants in urban areas were among the first to pay attention to interfamily ayuda. For example, one of the best descriptions of these practices can be found in Larissa Lomnitz's (1977) study conducted in a shantytown in Mexico City. Probably because of the lack of an ethnographic record on the topic in rural areas, she interprets it as an emergent response to difficult urban conditions rather than as something that the migrants brought with them.

More recently, perhaps because of the decline of either individually sponsored fiestas in many parts of Mesoamerica (Stephen 1991:178) or researchers' interest in them, anthropologists have paid a bit more attention to interfamily ayuda, usually conceptualizing it as a form of mutual aid. For example, Lynn Stephen's (1991) and Jeffrey Cohen's (1999) discussions of *guelaguetza* exchanges in Oaxacan villages appear to be what people in the Texcoco region would refer to as exchanges of ayuda. However, in these authors' treatments of the Oaxacan case, guelaguetza is understood to be about the objects exchanged:

> The primary purpose of in-kind guelaguetza is to allow a household, and women in particular, to prepare in advance for future ritual responsibilities. The principle of guelaguetza is to plan debts slowly and to recall them all at once to help finance major ritual events. The system allows women carefully to stock what they will need for a particular event by having loans planted with other people for particular items such as corn, beans, tortillas, bread, cacao, sugar, chiles, pigs, turkeys, and chickens, which they can recall as needed in conjunction with a specific event. (Stephen 1991:33)

Cohen likewise understands guelaguetza as a form of mutual aid for putting on fiestas. However, demonstrating his usual laudable willingness to admit when his informants' interpretations differ from his own, he states that only six of the twenty-five informants who said that they participate regularly in these exchanges mention "the goal or ideal of mutual support. . . . The remaining nineteen men stated that their participation was expected and so they participated" (1999:92). I suspect that these "expectations" are more significant than they appear in this quotation, in that these men are referring to the fact that fiestas are supposed to be put on this way, involving others, whether or not one needs the material objects exchanged. In what follows, I present the approach to interfamily ayuda that led me to such a suspicion.

According to López Millán (2008), residents of the pueblo of Santa Catarina del Monte in the sierra of the Texcoco region divide ayuda given for fiestas into two main categories: first, ayuda done with the hands, or *tlapalehuitl*, which refers to people physically helping with the preparations for the fiesta; and second, ayuda in kind, or *tlapalehuilizque*, in which objects are given for the fiesta. These two types of actions, while distinct, have two important characteristics in common, and I would add that these two characteristics are also common to the practice of participación described in the previous chapter. First, it is notable that these practices begin with an important and sometimes prolonged process of "inviting" someone to help. And second, in both cases, the ayuda given, whether in the form of work or an object, is inseparable from the donor him- or herself, so that what is really circulating in these practices are persons. I will discuss both of these characteristics in more detail below.

It is interesting to note that the provision of these two types of ayuda is actually considered part of the fiesta. López Millán (2008) posits that what we usually think of as a "fiesta," that is, the celebration where people sit down and eat, drink, and listen to music, is for people in Santa Catarina just the tip of the iceberg. Catarinos do not distinguish between what we would call the preparation for the festivity and the festivity itself and instead say that the fiesta begins when the organizers start to invite others *a ayudar* (to help). This process can start as much as a year ahead of time.

Tlapalehuitl: Ayuda Done with the Hands

Tlapalehuitl usually refers to food preparation for a fiesta and principally involves women rather than men. In the days leading up to the fiesta, women prepare the main dishes, usually chicken in mole sauce and either barbacoa or carnitas, accompanied by tortillas and *tlacoyos* (López Millán 2008).[3] Men do perform some work with their hands during this period: they may construct a wood-burning stove, slaughter animals, bring materials such as wood from higher up the mountainside, and help out moving heavy objects such as containers filled with water and pots of food (López Millán 2008). The men who help in this manner are usually the organizers' sons and sons-in-law or, if the organizers' children are too young, then their brothers and brothers-in-law. These men are part of or were recently part of the same nuclear family, so that the ayuda given is not clearly distinguishable from the daily, non-fiesta-related, intrafamilial exchanges of ayuda that I discuss below. No formal petition is required for these men to help. Rather, it is assumed that they will do so.

There are many more women than men who help, however. Some of these are also daughters and daughters-in-law whose ayuda is basically indistinguishable from their daily exchanges as members of the same nuclear family. These women help in the preparation of the main dish and tortillas but can also do a wider variety of tasks. However, there are usually fifteen to twenty women providing tlapalehuitl who are not immediate family members and only work in the preparation of the main dish and the tortillas.

These women, like the men, can also be divided into two categories. The first includes cousins, neighbors, and friends of the woman organizer, usually of her same generation, whom she has invited. The second are women who have been invited to help by a woman whom López Millán refers to as *una persona clave* (a key person). The organizer invites the key person, who in turn invites other women, who are indebted to the key person for having helped them in the past. The organizer who invites the key person will in turn be invited by the latter to help in the future for other fiestas. The women whom the key person brings to help are always from the same village and thus may be the organizers' distant cousins, friends, acquaintances, or neighbors, although this is not necessarily the case. What is certain is that all of these women, including the key person herself, will not receive any monetary compensation and will perform these activities *con gusto* (willingly; with enthusiasm). While women often measure the success of a fiesta by how many other women help, they do not make a distinction between helpers invited directly by the organizer and helpers invited by a key person. López Millán points out that an organizer is seen to have done a poor job in putting on the fiesta if she lacks women *para ayudar* (to help) or hires people to do the work.

These key persons, whom Catarinos themselves do not have a term for and just refer to by their names or as *abuelitas* (literally, grandmother, but in this case more a term of respect), occupy, I believe, a position analogous to a man who is *reconocido* (recognized) for his successful work as a mayordomo. Both of these "types" are recognized for their ability to mobilize a large number of people to *participar*, in the case of the mayordomo, or to *ayudar*, in the case of the key persons. As discussed in the previous chapter, a mayordomo achieves this by showing himself to be willing to work hard for others, performing this work con gusto and thus reminding people of the enjoyment in doing things together, and demonstrating his need for others. From what I have observed of "abuelitas" in Tepetlaoxtoc and from my reading of López Millán, being a key person is achieved in more or less the same manner. These women work alongside of the others—they do not simply direct or give orders. Plus, as I note above, this "work" does not have the negative connotation usually associated with the term but rather is part of the fiesta and is performed con gusto, and what is considered most enjoyable is working alongside the other women. Furthermore, while the other women are indebted to the abuelita for the ayuda they received from her in the past, the latter does not get them to help as an obligation by calling in their debts. Rather, she asks for their ayuda, emphasizing that she needs them and that they will be working together. Thus while these people are important—or "key," to use López Millán's term—they, like the mayordomos, are not powerful in the sense of having control over other people. They mobilize others by bringing out their subjectivity, not by approaching them as objects. And their own subjectivity is not that of the individual capable of acting on her own. Rather, they only act when invited to so by the organizer of a fiesta. It would not make sense for someone to go around offering herself as a key person for fiestas.

Tlapalehuilizque: Ayuda Given in Kind

López Millán (2008) divides *tlapalehuilizque*, or ayuda given in kind for a fiesta, into three different categories: (1) objects given as "gifts" as a part of long-term exchanges, so that there is no immediate agreement regarding their return; (2) objects given with a verbal agreement regarding their future return; and (3) objects given through a relationship of *padrinazgo* (godparenthood). The first category of action is usually performed only among closely related family members. For example, a grown but unmarried son or daughter will give it to his or her parents for a fiesta for a younger sibling or grown and married brothers and sisters will help each other in such a manner for their children's fiestas. This ayuda is often given in the form of cash, but it can also take the form of a performance by a musical band. Many Catarinos are musicians who earn money by playing in bands at fiestas, and if the person putting on the fiesta has a brother in a band, the latter can give this performance as a "gift" of this kind.[4] It is important to note that in this form of ayuda given in kind "the gift enters into a dynamic of return, but this dynamic is not established through a previous verbal agreement" (López Millán 2008:146; my translation). Rather, among these closely related family members there exists a relationship consisting of a general and long-term exchange of ayuda that goes beyond *tlapalehuilizque* and fiestas, so that there is no precise accounting of the quantity and kind of objects exchanged. (I discuss this kind of general, long-term exchange below in the section on intrafamilial ayuda.)

In the second type of ayuda given in kind, the two parties reach a verbal agreement of what is to be given for the imminent fiesta and what is to be returned when the donor throws a fiesta in the future. Here, the parties may be close family members such as brothers and sisters, but these kinds of arrangements are more frequently found among cousins, friends, and neighbors. Objects given may include animals for slaughter, soft and hard beverages, or disposable plates and cups, and the return agreed upon may be the exact same object or something equivalent in monetary value (López Millán 2008).

López Millán's (2008) third type of ayuda given in kind refers to a situation when a person or, more commonly, a married couple gives something for a fiesta as *padrinos* (godparents). The godparents for a baptism, known as *padrinos de velación*, pay for the mass and for the child's clothing for the ceremony. In the case of a wedding, the godparents pay for the rings, the mass, and the bride's dress. In minor *padrinazgos*, the godparents may pay for specific objects such as the video, photos, music, or flowers or for the mass for less significant celebrations such as school graduations. In contrast to other kinds of ayuda for fiestas, the padrinos will not have their prestation returned when they put on a fiesta later on. What the organizers of the fiesta do provide to the padrinos is a formal and extended invitation to participate that can even involve giving gifts to the padrinos in the case of important celebrations such as baptism and weddings. The organizers and the children for whom they are organizing the fiesta (the godchildren) must also treat the godparents *con respeto* (with respect) before, during, and after the fiesta.

Ayuda as Interdependent Action

As mentioned above, one of the things that tlapalehuitl and tlapalehuilizque have in common is that both begin with the organizer of the fiesta doing something to provoke the potential helper to agree to provide ayuda. In the case of tlapalehuitl, the woman organizing the fiesta visits a woman she intends to invite at the latter's house. López Millán describes one such interaction she observed between two cousins (2008:103–4). The woman extending the invitation, Mercedes, approaches the house of her cousin Jazmín and calls out to her with a wide smile on her face. Jazmín invites her inside to sit, and Mercedes makes polite conversation for a few minutes before stating that she and her husband want to prepare a *molito* (the dish to be served at the fiesta) for their kids' first communion in a couple of weeks. She then says, "¡Vengo a invitarte para que me eches la mano! ¿Cómo ves?" ("I've come to invite you so that you lend me a hand! What do you think?") (2008:104). Jazmín does not yet accede but instead just lifts her eyebrows, presses her lips together and responds, "Hmmmm . . . ¿Ya tan pronto?" ("Hmmmm . . . So soon already?") (2008:104), and Mercedes continues talking for another half an hour about the other women who are going to help. It is only when Mercedes gets up to leave that Jazmín says with a smile on her face, "¡Cómo no, Mercedes, allá nos vemos!" ("Of course, Mercedes, we'll see each other there!") (2008:104).

I have included this detailed description of this interaction because I agree with López Millán's observation that this is a key moment in the practice of tlapalehuitl and not "just" an invitation, and also because it recalls so clearly the verbal exchanges between the mayordomo and a potential participant described in the previous chapter. In both cases, the person in charge of putting on the fiesta takes an active role and visits the home of the potential "helper." The latter does not at first agree to help but instead allows the organizer to convince them. One of the points used in this convincing is that the organizer is recruiting or has already recruited others to help or participate, thus showing that he or she is taking the role seriously and that the fiesta will truly be put on "entre todos." It is important to remember that this coaxing occurs despite the fact that the potential helper is likely already indebted to the organizer and despite the fact that helping or participating is something that people want to do. In the case of the fiestas for the saints, people want to participate because of their relationship to the saint and because doing the fiesta "entre todos" is considered enjoyable. Meanwhile, in the case of tlapalehuitl, helping to prepare the food among others is also considered enjoyable and, as López Millán argues, providing ayuda is a manner in which Catarinos produce value, a point I will return to shortly. Thus, it is not surprising that once Jazmín accedes, she does so without any sign of reluctance. Yet the whole coaxing process is necessary because the potential helper needs the organizer to make her (or him) into an acting subject. *Hacer entre todos* (doing things together), like the fiesta itself, begins with the invitation, or, in other words, begins with the organizer's efforts to create active subjects. People are dependent on each other not just to put on fiestas but to begin to act.

If we are to understand the process of the invitation, we also have to understand what it means for people to say that, as with participation in mayordomías, tlapalehuitl is both obligatory and voluntary. It is obligatory because this is the way that fiestas are put on and people expect others to help. Vera Regehr, for example, cites an informant as saying, "Pues así es la costumbre, si ya me invitaron tengo que ir a ayudar, no importa si tengo trabajo, tengo que ir" ("Well, that's the custom, if they invited me then I have to go and help, it doesn't matter if I have work to do, I have to go") (2005:166). It is important to note that "obligatory" refers not to something that goes on in the invitation process itself but to something more general: "custom." When people say that helping is voluntary, in contrast, they are referring to the specific occasion, in relation to which they say that they help because they want to. The coaxing of the invitation is not meant to get people to feel obligated to do something against their will. Rather, it is what people need to be able to act and thus do what they want. Another quotation recorded by Regehr demonstrates this point: "Aquí así nos ayudamos, nos vienen a rogar para que podemos ir" ("Here we help each other in this manner, they come to plead with us so that we *can* go") (2005:166; my emphasis). People plead with others, not so that they *have* to go but so that they *can* go and help.

In the case of tlapalehuilizque, the form that the organizer's provocation takes depends on the type of ayuda in kind being exchanged. In the case of objects given as part of long-term exchanges, the donor sometimes appears to give the ayuda without any sort of provocation, but this may be because the provocation occurred at some point in the past when the organizer helped the donor in some manner. Such exchanges usually occur between close family members such as parents and children or siblings, so that they blend into the flow of the constant, long-term exchanges among these family members (López Millán 2008:145; see section below on intrafamilial ayuda). In contrast, when the objects given are with an expectation of a return, there is an immediate provocation, and it occurs in a relatively informal manner, contained within the negotiation over what will be given now and later. For example, one brother says to another, "Préstame seis cajas de refrescos y cuando tengas tu compromiso te las devuelvo" ("Lend me six cases of soft drinks and when you have your commitment [fiesta] I'll return them") (López Millán 2008:82).

For the case of padrinazgo, the organizer must make a formal petition to the potential padrinos. When asking a couple to be the godparents of the mass for a wedding, the bride and groom make an initial visit to the formers' home, talk about their plans to marry, and make their request (López Millán 2008:152). If the future godparents give an initial acceptance, then the bride and groom must return a week later with their parents and a basket with bread, fruit, and wine for the godparents. With this exchange, the bride and groom "secure" the couple as their godparents for the wedding. However, as López Millán states, additional visits may be necessary until the godparents have paid for everything they are supposed to (2008:152). López Millán also points out that if this procedure is not followed and the organizers petition the padrinos informally, it sometimes occurs that the padrinos back out, forcing the organizers into the undesirable position at the last minute of having to pay for part of the fiesta themselves (2008:157–58). I would say that through an informal petition, the organizers are conveying an attitude that they are not really so in need of others.

This implies doing a poor job of showing the padrinos that they are committed to doing the fiesta "entre todos" and of making the padrinos into active subjects. I would also add that while anthropologists have generally conceptualized padrinazgo in terms of the creation of social relations, I believe that the necessity of including padrinos in a fiesta has more to do with the principle of interdependence, or of doing things together. That is, padrinos are a formal and visible demonstration of the organizers' need of others. To put on a fiesta without padrinos is analogous to family members bearing the coffin of one of their own at a funeral. I think that in general, people in the region are not really concerned with forming relationships or expanding their social networks. The real problem is *hacer las cosas bien* (to do things in the correct manner), which means doing them entre todos. Social relationships are simply how this is made to happen. It could be said that relationships or networks are channels through which flows what really matters and what has to be produced: interdependent action and subjectivity.

The Inalienability of Ayuda

Another thing that tlapalehuitl and tlapalehuilizque have in common, apart from both requiring an invitation or provocation to occur, is that the ayuda given, whether in the form of work or an object, is inseparable from the donor, so we could say that what is really circulating in these practices are persons. In the previous chapter, I discuss how for people in Tepetlaoxtoc, the important thing about the mayordomía is not just putting on the fiesta for the saint but getting people to participate so that the fiesta "se hace entre todos." Similarly, in Santa Catarina del Monte, López Millán found that the success of life-cycle celebrations and the mayordomo's meals is measured in ayuda or the persons involved and not in terms of things that constitute what happens on the day of the celebration itself (i.e., the quantity and quality of the food, music, etc.). She notes that she figured out that the correct question to ask after a fiesta is "¿Qué tal le fue de ayuda?" ("How did you do in terms of help?"), rather than "¿Qué tal estuvo la fiesta?" ("How was the fiesta?") (2008:67). In fact, what happens on the day of the fiesta and the amount and kind of ayuda received are connected, since, as López Millán explains, most of the attendees consist of the people who have provided tlapalehuilizque and their families, the women who provide tlapalehuitl and their families, and people whom these women invite. These women even receive their invitees at the entrance and act as the hosts for these invitees as if the fiesta were theirs. Thus, a fiesta for which the organizers have received no or little ayuda will be poorly attended, or if the organizers somehow manage to get people to come, the guests will be poorly received because the organizers will have to receive all the guests themselves.

On one occasion in Tepetlaoxtoc, I ended up right in the middle of this second kind of problem along with my wife and some of my students. A middle-aged couple without children who had lived in Mexico City for many years took on the mayordomía of the Santísima Trinidad. I imagine that because of their childlessness and their lack of ties to people in the village they received little ayuda for the meal they had to provide as mayordomos. The day before the meal, we were asking the mayordomos about the fiesta and when the subject of the meal came up, they asked my wife, some students, and me if we would be willing to help serve it. Thinking it would be a good opportunity to observe a fiesta from the ayuda end of things, we accepted. A good number of people showed up, but few of them hid the fact that they were unhappy with the attention they were receiving. I believe this had little to do with our service in and of itself and more to do with the fact that they received little personal attention from their hosts. If the mayordomos had prepared the meal with ayuda from other women in the village, they would have had help hosting as well, and every guest would have received personal attention from the person who had invited them.

As we can see, providing tlapalehuitl is not just about giving ayuda in the form of work but about being part of the fiesta itself. The same could be said of those providing tlapalehuilizque, even though their physical presence is not quite so obvious. López Millán notes that Catarinos speak of these prestations in terms of the people and not the objects given, stating, for example, that what they are giving is *compañía* (company) or that they are doing it to *acompañar* (accompany) the organizers (2008:78). She adds that the whole anthropological tendency of dividing up these kinds of practices into moments of giving, receiving, and returning objects distracts our attention from what really matters: people accompanying each other. In other words, "the objects are just a vehicle for involving more people" (2008:87; my translation). Similarly, in his discussion of padrinazgo in the village of San Juan Tezontla, located approximately halfway between Tepetlaoxtoc and Santa Catarina, Junior Encarnación Ruiz posits that the material objects exchanged are not what really matters. Instead, "the people of San Juan Tezontla dedicate a considerable part of their time to inviting and bringing in others to reciprocal relationships *to do things together*. From introducing a newborn into the social life of the village to constructing a new home and organizing the village's whole population, up to a burial, *they must do everything together; they should not do anything alone*" (2004:100; my emphases and translation).

Ayuda as Person-Value

López Millán discusses the importance Catarinos place on this "doing things together" in terms of value. She notes that villagers talk about the abundance of ayuda in terms of *riqueza* (wealth) and say that those who lack it are *pobres* (poor people) even if they are rich in material terms (2008:67). She then goes on to suggest that the act of ayudar produces value—a value she refers to as "person-value" in contrast to the "object-value" of capitalism. This is not to say that Catarinos do not participate in the creation of "object-value"; rather, this is not the only kind of value in the village and probably not the most important for most people. Drawing on Nancy Munn's (1986) conceptualization of value production in Gawa, Melanesia, López Millán posits that Catarinos produce value by giving things to others rather than consuming things themselves. This can include work: they produce value by working to prepare the food in a fiesta instead of working to make money for themselves. As in Gawa, when people give things to others the things are not alienated from them but instead extend their person to others. In other words, the things people give in Santa Catarina—including material objects, work, and even speech (in the invitations)—are not just an excuse for what we would think of as a process of forming relationships. Rather, these things are a vehicle through which people literally extend themselves to others, thereby accompanying them.

A comparison to our own notions of value production may prove useful. We could say that we see ourselves as creating value by working to produce objects. This value is then activated or converted into something useful for the producer in one of two kinds of exchange: first, by giving things away and receiving, in return for our friendly selflessness, a social connection; and second, selling things and receiving material wealth. This kind of value production, even when finalized through a gift, can be considered "object-value," to use López Millán's term, since the value is contained in the objects themselves and they must be alienated from the producer to fulfill their potential as value. In contrast, people in the Texcoco region create "person-value" by extending themselves through the things given; nothing is really given away. We could say that creating person-value is about producing subjects rather than objects in the sense that the important thing about giving objects to others is that the giving itself constitutes subjectivity or action. Here too, this value must be activated, but in this case it is activated *by* another and not *through* another. The person organizing the fiesta and doing the inviting allows or causes the invitee to act, but the action and the value are inseparable from the invitee. Thus, it is difficult to say who creates the value; it would probably be most accurate to say both parties collaborate and create the value together. Also, while the people organizing the fiesta could be said to be wealthy with ayuda, they cannot really possess this wealth: it not only belongs to the invitees, it *is* the invitees in the form of active subjects. And while these invitees could be said to accumulate this ayuda or value and later turn it into wealth when others help them, this second round of wealth will also belong to and be their invitees.

Intrafamily Ayuda

Prestations of ayuda can also be found among members of the same family, as I have already mentioned, mainly in the form of intergenerational exchanges. Husbands and wives may sometimes exchange ayuda, but more often they function as a complementary unit in relation to their children. Parents provide ayuda to their sons and daughters in the form of care and nurturance when they are young and then, later on, by helping to pay for their wedding and bequeathing them land to build a house on, often when the parents are still alive. Children, meanwhile, help their parents by working to contribute to the family economy. This involves doing chores around the house as soon as they are able. Boys and girls as young as two or three can be found removing corn kernels from the cob, sweeping the floor, or feeding chickens (Magazine and Ramírez Sánchez 2007:57). In their early teens, they begin to help with extradomestic tasks as well, accompanying their fathers to construction sites after school, for example, or working sewing machines in family workshops. Starting in their late teens and until they get married, many sons and daughters get full- or part-time wage-paying jobs and contribute the majority of their earnings to their parents as ayuda. Up until the mid-1980s in the Texcoco region, this usually meant that teenage sons and daughters went to Mexico City to find work either as domestic servants or as helpers in a wide variety of businesses such as market stalls, restaurants, and workshops. They would return to their villages once every week or two to deliver most of their pay to their parents as ayuda.

This pattern of giving ayuda begins to change when sons or daughters marry.[5] When I refer to "marriage," I am using the term in its local sense, which refers to a decision to marry (*casarse*) and live together without necessarily having a civil or religious ceremony right away. If, when they marry, sons or daughters are able to set up an economically independent neolocal residence, then they will likely cease to give ayuda to their parents. But even after they cease to give ayuda, if this is the case, they still expect to receive ayuda from their parents in the form of inheritance in land and to pay for their church wedding if and when they decide to have one. However, they will likely resume giving ayuda to their parents when the latter need care in their old age. These exchanges can even continue after their parents' deaths as sons and daughters care for the souls of their departed parents (Downing 1973; González Montes 1992), and in exchange their dead parents may petition the saints and God on their behalf (Good Eshelman 2004b).

Other sons and daughters, because of economic limitations, are not able to set up a neolocal residence when they marry and thus take up residence with the groom's parents. If this is the case, the newlyweds usually continue to provide ayuda to the groom's parents in the form of helping with work around the house or contributing part or most of their wages to the family economy. They will usually also try to put aside some of their earnings to gradually achieve economic and residential independence. I say that this achievement is gradual, because people commonly separate one aspect of the family economy at a time. For example, the young couple may begin by building a separate bedroom onto the groom's parents' house. Then, when they have saved up a bit more money or have increased their earning capacity, they may build a separate kitchen, thus separating their food budget from that of the rest of the residential group. With each of these steps, the couple decreases their dependence on the groom's parents and thus also justifies contributing less ayuda. We could say that with each step they decrease their interdependence with the groom's parents. Finally, when they have saved up enough money and, usually, have inherited a plot of land from the groom's parents, they build their own dwelling, thus completing the separation.

This separation is not necessarily measurable in spatial terms, because the inherited land is often a part of the same plot where the groom's parents have their house. Also, it is not absolute, because as already noted, the exchanges of ayuda will continue when the couple has a church wedding if they have not already done so, and they help the groom's parents in old age. Additionally, when the groom's parents or one of his brothers takes on a mayordomía or when one of his brothers or sisters marries or baptizes a child, then the separated households may temporarily help each other in a manner reminiscent of their former everyday interdependence. That is, they may give ayuda in a more generalized manner, without the specific accounting of what is given and received that occurs in exchanges of tlapalehuitl or tlapalehuilizque among more-distant relatives, friends, and neighbors. This separation is not absolute in another sense as well: the independence achieved is only in relation to the groom's parents, since one of the main objectives of this separation is for the couple to direct their ayuda to their own children to foment a new relationship of interdependence with this next generation (see Regehr 2005).

This latter pattern of newlyweds continuing to live with and give ayuda to the groom's parents could be considered the norm among officially and unofficially indigenous people throughout Mesoamerica (Robichaux 1997, 2005b). However, at least in the case of Tepetlaoxtoc, the first pattern, that of neolocal postmarital residence, was quite common from the 1950s to the 1980s because of the availability of relatively high paying and stable jobs in Mexico City. A good number of young people from Tepetlaoxtoc met and married people from elsewhere or got together with someone they already knew from the village while working in Mexico City. It was still common, however, for these couples to send some ayuda to their parents in the village, and one of the reasons for this was to keep open the possibility of returning at some point to have a church wedding there or to live on inherited land. As discussed in chapter 2, this return to inherited land was forced upon many people with the economic crises and neoliberal reforms of the 1980s and 1990s. In recent years, because more people work in the Texcoco region or commute daily to Mexico City, the pattern of newlyweds taking up patrilocal postmarital residence is once again common.

The Economics of Survival or the Production of Active Subjects?

The different stages of the development cycle of domestic groups tend to each produce particular economic conditions (see Magazine and Ramírez Sánchez 2007). When a couple first marries and before they have children, they can both work, and they have few expenses, so saving money or beginning their gradual separation from the groom's parents is relatively easy. However, this working, saving, and separating are all usually in anticipation of having children. Once they have children who at a young age receive ayuda but return none or little, a difficult economic stage begins.

Then, when the children are a bit older and begin to contribute ayuda, the economic strain lessens. It lessens still more in the stage when sons and daughters, as young unmarried adults, need almost nothing from their parents and contribute most of their earnings—often from full-time jobs—as ayuda to their parents. This surplus will allow the parents to help pay for their sons' and daughters' weddings.

These oscillations in the family's economic situation through the development cycle of the domestic group are undoubtedly significant to the actors involved, but I do not want to give the impression that these exchanges are just about economics or financial need. For one thing, as Good Eshelman shows (2005:284), these exchanges seem to increase rather than decrease with prosperity. Furthermore, as in the case of mayordomías and ayuda for fiestas, local actors conceptualize the exchanges in terms of interdependence and the importance of doing things together. As Ángela Velásquez Velásquez notes in her study of young people and family in the Texcocan village of San Juan Tezontla, *hacer las cosas juntos* (doing things together) is what people mean when they refer to *hacerlo bien* (2007:58). People do not see poverty as the reason for these exchanges, but rather the fact that people need each other in a basic manner: *nunca están completos* (they are never complete) (Regehr 2005:144). In fact, as occurs in tlapalehuilizque, people speak of these exchanges in terms of the people involved and not the objects exchanged. They use phrases such as *estar juntos* (being together) or *trabajar juntos* (working together) and *estar aparte* (being apart) (Regehr 2005; see also Good Eshelman 2005). Being or working together here need not refer to physical proximity. Rather, the exchanges are what constitute the togetherness. As with ayuda for fiestas (discussed above), it is useful to think of the ayuda sons and daughters give to their parents as inalienable, that is, as a part of themselves that they are extending through these prestations and thus creating togetherness.[6] Thus, if sons and daughters who work in other parts of Mexico or in the United States send remittances back to their parents, they are all "together." Rather than boasting about their material wealth in and of itself, parents like to talk about how their sons and daughters work together with them. The sons and daughters and their work, their action, or their subjectivity are what matter.

While, as noted above, couples with young children often struggle financially, such families are not pitied locally, because their children's current and future work and ayuda constitutes their wealth. Pitied would be childless couples, but not because of a lack of object wealth, since without young children as dependents they can live well in a material sense. Rather, they are to be pitied because life loses a good part of its meaning because *están solos* (they are alone) without anyone for them to make into son and daughter subjects by giving ayuda or to make them into father or mother subjects by receiving it. Childless couples or parents who do not have a close relationship to their children, for whatever reason, are even referred to as being "poor," whether or not they are lacking in terms of material wealth. A formalized marriage without children is likewise somewhat meaningless, which may be one reason why couples usually wait a few years to consolidate their marriage through a church wedding, at which time they usually have children. In the first years of my research, before my son was born, villagers usually looked puzzled upon hearing that my wife and I were formally married but did not yet have children.

Marriage is about having children; being a husband or wife is about being a father or mother; and being a child is about being a son or daughter. However, it is also important to note that being a mother, father, son, or daughter is constituted by the action of providing ayuda to the members of the other generation. In other words, being a mother, father, son, or daughter is not simply a state based on biologically or legally defined relations but rather a subjectivity or form of action that must be achieved through that action. Thus, we could say that the point of giving ayuda is to achieve these subjectivities and also to achieve togetherness, since the ayuda that is given is inalienable and thus constitutes togetherness. In contrast, I would say that in the modern West, we often see identities such as mother, father, son, and daughter as biological givens, leaving action to be directed toward other ends. More specifically, when writing as anthropologists about campesinos or other "poor" people in Mexico, we often imagine that the action of exchanging ayuda is about the things exchanged and about security or survival in material terms. It is rarely considered that such actions constitute being a parent, son, or daughter (but see Good Eshelman 2005).

Lourdes Arizpe (1980), for example, makes precisely this argument in relation to sons' and daughters' migration from rural Mexican villages to cities to work. She sees these migrations as "a strategy of campesino families to survive and reproduce themselves when faced with the economic pressure of the industrial capitalist sector" (1980:5; my translation). This strategy involves what she calls "relay migration" (*migración por relevos*), in which one family member migrates and sends home money to support the others until the next family member is old enough to take his place. After a couple's first child is born and the family enters the precarious economic stage I described above, the father migrates first, to be followed by the oldest child when he or she reaches the age of about fourteen. That child can then return to the village a few years later and marry when the next-to-oldest sibling takes his or her place, and so on. Arizpe calculates that a family needs three or four children to cover their economic needs during this stage of the development cycle, although more children are better because they allow for an accumulation of surplus that can be invested in the youngest children's education. Moreover, Arizpe imagines the campesino family as an economic unit, which is reflected in her idea that this relay migration constitutes a family strategy for survival: "In a campesino society the members of a family do not act following individualistic norms, but rather in relation to the domestic group. Within this group, in general, it is the patriarch who exercises the power of decision—sometimes in consultation with his wife—about how the division of labor within the family enterprise will occur and who will leave [the community]" (1980:14).

I would not disagree that sons' and daughters' work allows for "survival" and that the father, sometimes in consultation with his wife, makes decisions so as to coordinate everyone's actions. However, I also think that this emphasis on economics and on the family as a unit misses the point of what is really going on from a local perspective. As I have already stated, sons' and daughters' migration, work, and remittances are about achieving son- and daughterhood as subjectivities and about achieving togetherness. Furthermore, children are hardly objects in an adult strategy concerned with obtaining the material wealth necessary for biological and social survival, as Arizpe portrays them. Parents do indebt children by giving them ayuda in the form of care and nurturance, but this is intended not to control their children but rather to provoke them to act as subjects. Parents do state that sons and daughters must work, but by this they mean that that is what being a son or daughter is: they must do it because it is their "custom." They are also careful to point out that they do not force their children to do anything and that being together is voluntary. Sons and daughters are quite clear on the fact that the work they have done constitutes their ayuda—their parents do not appropriate their actions even if the fruits of these actions end up in the parents' hands. Both parents and children are also quite clear that the parents owe them something in return for their ayuda. Regehr quotes a mother talking about her five-year-old daughter: "First she must work, so that her father builds her a house. If one day she marries and her husband doesn't have anything, then she will already have at least a room. But first she must work, so that she earns it" (Regehr 2005:143; my translation). And we can add that the parents need their sons and daughters to act voluntarily and as subjects because the provocation of their children is what then causes them to continue acting as mothers and fathers.

From the local point of view then, the family is "together" not because it functions as a unit whose members form an indistinguishable whole but because people extend themselves to others through their ayuda. The idea of an indistinguishable whole is also contradicted by the fact that this togetherness looks different from the point of view of parents versus children. For the former, it means sons and daughters working on their behalf, and this ayuda received constitutes their own person-value wealth. But this same wealth also belongs to the sons and daughters who give it, and for them while it represents a current togetherness, it also contains the seed of their future separation (Regehr 2005:160). The ayuda they give to their parents is also their own, and in the future it will cause their parents to provide them with a wedding and inheritance, thus making their separation possible.

I believe that many children who *are* treated as objects by their parents enact a separation through migrations to cities. For example, in Tepetlaoxtoc, a man of about fifty told me the story of how he left home to go to Mexico City at the age of nine because his father drank too much and beat him. For a few years he slept in bus or train stations or doorways and sold newspapers and candy. One day a woman asked if he wanted to come work for her in a store, and it turned out that she was also from Tepetlaoxtoc. They took good care of him, and he ended up working for them for nineteen years. He said that their care changed his life completely and during this time he started sending back money to help his mother and bringing his brothers to the city to find them jobs. If he had not received this ayuda, he would have continued to live as what are known as *niños de la calle*, or "street children."

My own earlier research on so-called street children suggested that these people might best be understood as sons and daughters who have separated themselves from their families in rural areas. These eight- to twenty-five-year-old migrants to the city from rural areas, who live in abandoned buildings, sewers, and cheap hotels, are often seen to be in need of aid because they lack the caretaking and socialization of adults (Magazine 2003b). I believe, however, that their problem is not this lack of caretaking or socialization but rather the lack of social relations and exchanges of ayuda that constitute subjectivity and give life meaning in the villages from which they come (Magazine 2003a, 2004). If they are not somehow reintegrated into exchange relationships as in the case of the man described above, they usually attempt to re-create something of these relationships by forming *bandas* (gangs), which are somewhat analogous to the village community or to the people who exchange ayuda for fiestas, and by marrying and having children with fellow "street kids." These re-creations seem to work to an extent to give life meaning, but I think that their disconnectedness, aloneness (not loneliness), or incompleteness are still felt and may be what cause their often-excessive drug and alcohol use.

Family as a Site for Reproduction or as a Site for Exchanging Ayuda?

In general, what I would like to suggest here in this section on intrafamily ayuda is that we may usefully conceptualize family in Texcoco and similar regions as being "about" these exchanges. Similar to practices of interfamily ayuda, these exchanges may concern the things given, but mostly, they are about the creation of mother, father, son, and daughter subjectivities and of togetherness, conceived as the extension of persons to others through prestations of ayuda. As has been argued (Collier and Yanagisako 1987; Schneider 1984; Strathern 1988, 1992), anthropologists often approach family or kinship with assumptions derived from their own modern Western notions about what these things mean. Briefly put, family is assumed to be where biological reproduction and a good part of social reproduction, in the form of socialization or the inculcation of society's rules and values, take place. Nature, not people, produces persons or subjects through biological reproduction. What people or, more specifically, parents do is to socialize children who are born into a state of nature. Or we could say that parents are in charge of disciplining and molding children's innate subjectivity. It is not that families are meant to turn children into objects—adults are undoubtedly supposed to have subjectivity—but this subjectivity is natural, it was already produced by nature, and the family's contribution takes the form of the object side of the person: society internalized through socialization.

I would not want to deny that family in the Texcoco region or other comparable areas involves biological reproduction and the learning of rules and values, although I hesitate to equate these rules and values with "society," since society in this case is, if it makes sense to use that term at all, primarily constituted by interdependence and the creation of subjects, not by a social contract among complete, independent persons. But if these biological and social reproductive processes do take place in the family, they do not occupy central stage. For example, the significant social unit is defined not by biology but by who exchanges ayuda, or in local terms who is "together" or "works together." According to Good Eshelman, "The Nahuas recognize kinship relations based on biology and marriage, but these are secondary to the conceptualization of the domestic group described here. There are cases in which people who share a residency have biological or matrimonial ties, but they belong to two or three distinct 'domestic groups.' There are also cases of a group that 'works together' but whose members live in two or three different houses" (2005:279; my translation). Furthermore, as Regehr (2005) has argued, the family as group and questions of group membership are not particularly of interest in local terms. In fact, it is not really clear that there is a "group" that people can have "membership" in. Togetherness is action and must be constantly re-created, which is why people can say that they are together one moment and then apart the next (Regehr 2005:153). Family is a site where this action may take place, but the primary objective of this action is not social reproduction. We could say, rather, that family is the site, or at least one of them, for reproducing not the social but rather action or subjectivity.

Additionally while the family may be where children are first introduced to exchanges of ayuda and where they learn to participate, this is not because it is the family's function to teach them this to prepare them to go out into the "real" social world beyond. Rather, children learn about these exchanges in the family because they are occurring all around the child, even involving him, as soon as he is born. Recall that the care a child receives from his parents and others is understood as ayuda—not just as a postnatal aspect of biological reproduction—and this ayuda indebts the child who is still unable to give anything in return (Good Eshelman 2005; Magazine and Ramírez Sánchez 2007; Regehr 2005). Thus, it could be said that children are born into a state of indebtedness or interdependency rather than into a state of nature (Good Eshelman 2005:288; Magazine and Ramírez Sánchez 2007). Duncan Earle, similarly, observes that "[t]he Quiché [Maya] are not born with original sin but rather 'original debt,' a debt to their ancestors who made their own existence possible and who gave them their piece of the material world" (1986:170). As Regehr shows, when children eventually begin to help their parents, the parents make comments such as "Ya se da cuenta" ("Now he gets it"), "Abren los ojos" ("They are opening their eyes") or "Apenas despiertan" ("They are just waking up") (2005:174). These comments suggest that when children's cognitive capacities have matured sufficiently they realize that they were social all along, where being social means being incomplete and thus in need of others (Regehr 2005:174–75). In other words, they wake up and see their sociality, but they do not have to be "socialized" from a supposedly natural individual state.

FIVE

Problems with "Ethnicity" and "Modernization"

The third and final topic I attempt to rethink, the ethnic relationship between indigenous people and modern or urban "mestizo" people, along with the intertwined question of the former's transformation into the latter, has been present since the first anthropological studies in Mexico (e.g., Gamio 1979 [1922]; Redfield 1930, 1970 [1941]). Since colonial times, it has also been a question of central importance to the state. This heavy focus on indigenous/European ethnic relations and processes of acculturation or modernization distinguishes the traditional anthropology of highland Mexico from that of other world regions such as Melanesia and Amazonia. Of course these regions have experienced and continue to experience colonialism, but the relative isolation of indigenous people in these regions has made it easier to ignore colonialism and contact with the modern world in anthropological studies, at least until recently. Neglect of this topic in these regions was obviously a problem, but on the positive side, the ease with which anthropologists ignored colonialism and state power enabled a more careful and complete focus on local ways of living and understanding life. In contrast, Mexico, and highland Latin America more generally, with their longer and more invasive colonial and national state rule, have contributed to the discipline as a whole in other ways, advancing our knowledge of the relationship between life at a local level and historical process, global capitalism, colonialism, and state power. However, this greater sensitivity to vertical relations has meant, I believe, sacrificing attention to how people live and understand their lives, at least in comparison to work done in Melanesia and Amazonia. Through a reflection on the topic of the relationship between the indigenous and the modern, I hope to suggest the necessity of combining these two approaches, which we might call horizontal and vertical, to ask how the people we study experience and understand these vertical (ethnic) relations and the process we usually think of as modernization. In other words, I believe that for the study of Mexico, and probably of many other places around the world, we need to combine attention to profoundly different ways of being human with a recognition of connectedness and contemporaneity. I propose that an exploration of local manners of approaching connectedness and contemporaneity contributes to this effort.

During the colonial period in Mexico, the Spaniards attempted, among other things, to Christianize and "civilize" indigenous people while carefully preserving the category of *"indio"* (Indian) for purposes of labor exploitation (Bonfil Batalla 1973). Since independence, two somewhat contradictory forces have been at work, with one or the other moving to the fore during different periods. On the one hand, the state has attempted to transform indigenous people into Mexicans or mestizos (mixed people) in local terms, since nationalist myth has it that Mexicans are a mix between Spanish and indigenous culture and blood. Overtly this is done for the good of the "backward" indigenous people to bring them the benefits of modern culture and citizenship. It also clearly constitutes part of a nation-building project and an effort to make indigenous people into subjects of the state and global capitalism. On the other hand, a national myth that values the country's indigenous past as what makes it unique encourages efforts to protect and display contemporary indigenous culture as a vestige of that past. Currently, a similar attitude dominates national policy, at least at a superficial level, toward indigenous people, in the form of multi- or interculturalism. Multi- or interculturalist discourse or policy claims to value indigenous culture as part of the present, even though, as I discuss below, truly bringing the so-called indigenous into the present is more difficult than it sounds. I state that the domination of this attitude may be superficial because what I have heard and observed informally about intercultural programs suggests that many of them attempt to integrate indigenous culture into educational programs not to truly transform what education is about but so that indigenous people more readily learn what they have to learn to access the benefits of the modern world. In other words, these policies are in reality veiled attempts to integrate indigenous people into modern Mexico.

Anthropologists interested in the topic of indigenous-modern relations have principally been concerned with how this process of modernization occurs or why it does not. Early studies, such as Robert Redfield's (1970 [1941]) work in the Yucatán Peninsula, assumed a gradual but steady process of assimilation or acculturation of indigenous people to modernity brought on by proximity and contact. Eric Wolf (1955) added resistance to this formula, suggesting how indigenous people maintain the boundaries of the closed corporate community to protect themselves from what they see as an exterior hostile world—although he concluded that it was only a matter of time before capitalism wore down community barriers, allowing acculturation to run its course. The Mexican anthropologist Gonzalo Aguirre Beltrán (1973 [1967]) showed that this hostile world was purposely maintained by local nonindigenous elites to maintain a relationship of domination similar to the one under colonialism. By denying neighboring indigenous people access to the benefits of modernity, local elites could secure a cheap supply of indigenous products and labor.

Aguirre Beltrán played an important role in formulating and implementing government programs aimed at breaking down local resistance to modernization. During the 1950s, '60s, and '70s, a large portion of Mexico's indigenous population was "modernized" through schools and other government programs that taught them Spanish and other skills necessary to avoid the stigma of indigenousness and to find temporary or permanent work in urban areas. However, another Mexican anthropologist, Guillermo Bonfil Batalla (1973), in his study of the industrialized and formerly indigenous city of Cholula, argued that this assimilation was deceptive. He described people who had superficially assimilated to national society to gain access to better jobs and to avoid prejudice. However, when it came to the values that truly defined their lives, they had remained indigenous and had done so because they were unable to compete successfully for prestige in the mestizo world.

Others have suggested that this "deceptive assimilation" has characterized indigenous Mesoamericans since colonial times and that it should be understood not simply as a response to domination but rather as a result of a particular manner of being in and understanding the world. Pedro Pitarch, for example, suggests that the following sixteenth-century observation regarding the Tupinambas of Brazil is also applicable to indigenous people in Mexico:

In an essay that treats the attraction of the Tupinambas of the 16th century for the Christian religion . . . Viveiros de Castro cites the Jesuit
Antonio Vieira, who, in questions related to doctrines of faith, distinguishes two types of nations. One that is naturally firm, obstinate, and
constant; they defend themselves, resist, argue, retort, even take up arms;
but once they have given up and accepted the faith, they maintain it
firmly and constantly. They are—Vieira says—like marble statues that
once finished require no more work. In contrast there are other nations,
like the Indians of Brazil, that accept everything they are told easily and
docilely; without arguing, doubting or resisting; but they are inconstant
and indifferent to the faith. They are like myrtle statues that, without the
gardener's clippers, lose their new appearance and return to their old and
natural brutishness. (2003b:71; my translation)

Gary Gossen, in turn, states, "Something must account for the capacity
of the Mesoamerican world, over the millennia, to generate tens of thou-
sands of symbolic representations of the social, natural, and supernatural
world which bear such a generic, isomorphic similarity that they remain
translatable and adaptive as political and economic circumstances change.
*Something must also account for the Mesoamerican capacity to assimilate
alien cultural forms and make them their own*" (1986:2; my emphasis). He
attempts to account for continuity by proposing the existence of a kind of
deep structure he calls "templates" or "generative principles" that then
produce "derivative phenomena." Alfredo López Austin (2001) suggests
something similar in his concept of the *núcleo duro* (hard nucleus), as does
Eva Hunt (1977) through her notion of "armature." Johanna Broda, meanwhile, focuses more on how to imagine change, which implies "conceiving
of indigenous cultural manifestations not as the direct and uninterrupted
continuity of the Prehispanic past nor as archaisms, but to visualize them in
a creative process of constant re-elaboration, sustained at the same time in
very remote roots" (2001:167; my translation). These proposals constitute
attempts to identify and address a pair of conundrums faced by anthropologists: first, how indigenous culture remains after five hundred years of
domination and acculturation; and second, how it can be that people who
seem so "modern" and similar to us can at the same time be so different,
which is one of my concerns here.[1]
    One thing that all of these formulations, from Redfield to Bonfil to Gos-
sen, have in common is an assumption that indigenousness and modernity
are "cultures" and thus things. When I say this, I am referring not to the

simple use of these terms but to the assumption that what defines groups of people and what makes them different from each other are the *things* that they have produced, including deep structures, and which constitute the particular social world in which they live. In other words, these authors, not unlike anthropologists in general (Wagner 1981 [1975]), conceptualize indigenousness and modernity and the relation between them in their own terms and assume that their informants do so as well.

I would like to suggest here that we will not fully understand ethnic relations or processes of continuity and change until we pay attention to our informants' understandings of self and otherness and how these understandings differ from our own.

Eduardo Viveiros de Castro provides a contrast that serves as a useful starting point for such a discussion: whereas for us the form of the other is the thing or the object, for "Amerindians" it is the person or the subject (2004:468). We, as anthropologists, usually provide what could be seen as a useful example of this first manner of recognizing the other. In order to "see" the people we study as other, we must find and describe the things they have produced beyond what we recognize as nature: their culture, their society, their history, their technology, and so forth. As Roy Wagner (1981 [1975]) points out, even if we do not find it we had better invent it for them or risk losing our bearings completely. In contrast, Amerindians can only recognize an other that is a person in the form of a subject. Aparecida Vilaça describes Amazonian encounters with other groups in such terms: "[F]ar from comprising primarily visual experiences (such as our own visits to museums and other places), journeys for Amazonian peoples involve the establishment of intense social relations and living (peaceful and otherwise) with people from these other worlds" (2010:315). Similarly, people from the Texcoco region, to recognize an other, need to encounter not culture but rather an interaction with other people that, specifically, they expect to take the form of the production of active subjectivity. As I demonstrate below, because people from the city tend to act on their own and to assume that others do the same, the region's residents tend to see them as lacking something basic, as foolish, or as unproductive. We could say that the region's residents are unable to see or recognize city people as an other at all because city people do not appear to be concerned with subjectivity and its production, and this is why the region's residents describe them in negative terms such as "foolish."[2]

This kind of alternative approach to otherness in Mesoamerica has begun to emerge in recent studies that suggest that indigenous people, when it comes to processes such as assimilation, may not be particularly concerned with *things* such as cultures or identities at all. Pitarch (2003b), for example, discusses how Tzeltal people in Chiapas show considerable enthusiasm for new ideas of external origin. One example of this is the manner in which they readily convert to one religion after another (see also Severi 2004). These conversions, seen as we usually understand such actions—that is, as the taking on of a new "identity" that defines the whole person or, I would add, as assimilation into a new cultural world—make these people appear unfaithful or superficial. Pitarch suggests, however, that something else is going on with these conversions. People see the different religions as values to be appropriated (2003b:69) and the conversions as a way to try out different manners of being (2003b:75) to see whether they have positive effects on health and well-being in general (2003b:69). What we would usually think of as culture contact or assimilation turns out to occur at the level of what we usually prefer not to change—what we might call the self or our way of being. Sounding very much like what Wagner (1981 [1975]) describes for "traditional" societies, people's actions are directed toward transforming or extending the person rather than their society or culture. I suggest that something similar is going on among residents of the Texcoco region, who see the city as a place where they can learn new ways of being that are useful for doing business and making money. By this learning, I refer not to something such as how to run a business but rather to how to "be" a boss or a subordinate—that is, how to relate to others hierarchically, through subjectivities that are considered foreign, although by no means new, to village life. Thus, modernity is seen not as a thing but as a subjectivity, and when villagers experience "modernization" or "urbanization," this constitutes not a cultural or social change but rather a change at the level of the person.

Beyond considering indigenous people as contemporaries and as intellectual equals, I believe that a conceptualization of a truly polyethnic society must take such alternative manners of approaching otherness into account. Policies based on multi- or interculturalism, at least ideally, are oriented toward the achievement of such an egalitarian polyethnic society, but, I believe, they are doomed to failure because they assume that the commonality among different groups is the production and possession of a particular "culture" built on a universal "nature." Thus, while it is undoubtedly true, as studies of cultural politics have shown (e.g., Friedlander 1975; Hernández Castillo 2001), that people in Mexico may invent an indigenous culture to make political claims, instead of having to do so because they lost this culture at some point in the past, I posit that this culture must be invented because it never existed at all as such. That is, they had never defined themselves in terms of the things—such as traditions, social structures, rituals, myths, and so forth—that they had produced and possessed, and so such a definition had to be invented for the sake of government agencies or other actors that do recognize an other through its culture. Therefore, "culture" is not the appropriate "inter" or bridge on which to base a polyethnic society that includes people who do not share our notions of culture, self, and otherness. I believe that we need to continue searching for the appropriate bridge. This quest will no doubt take time and effort, but before we can even begin, we need to see and accept that current dominant versions of otherness are not universal.

I think that when we approach a place such as Tepetlaoxtoc as anthropologists we usually imagine that people there are concerned with *culture* when, for example, they put on fiestas; that they are preoccupied with *ethnicity* when they try to prevent outsiders from settling in the village; or that they are interested in *modernizing* when they send their children to the city for education or when the latter bring home urban youth styles. I assumed these things when I began my research, and there appears to be evidence to support all three postulations. As we have seen, people in Tepetlaoxtoc dedicate significant time, energy, and money to fiestas, and they are also concerned with distinguishing themselves from people from the city and with putting up boundaries that discourage their settlement in the village. I have not given modernity much attention until now, but it would probably be the most striking feature of the Texcoco region to anyone familiar with more-isolated highland villages in other parts of Mexico. Tepetlaoxtoc, for example, appears to be almost completely modernized or urbanized with its paved streets, schools, Spanish monolinguism, and salaried, often skilled and well-educated, workers. We might say that even if the people of Tepetlaoxtoc have somewhat neglected the reproduction of their traditional culture, they have been diligent in their efforts to modernize.

What I would like to suggest here, however, is that things such as the traditional culture of fiestas and the modernization, which can all be found if we look for them, can also be understood as conduits or by-products of actions directed toward the production of active subjects. In this chapter, I try to work through this confusion between means, ends, and by-products by comparing how anthropologists and other "urbanites," on the one hand, and villagers, on the other, understand actions related to what I refer to as

fiestas (as a supposedly clear example of local "culture") and modernization. I also touch upon how villagers interpret urbanites' understandings.
These interpretations suggest that we are not the only ones to impose our
own thinking on others, even while the respective results of these two
impositions are quite different.

The Reproduction of Traditional Culture versus the Production of Active Subjects

In this section, I begin a discussion of contrasting versions of otherness
by returning to the divergent conceptualizations of fiestas and mayordomías discussed in chapter 3. I do so because villagers use the example
of how people from the city understand or, better said, misunderstand
mayordomías to develop their own theories about their urban neighbors.
While this reference to otherness and mayordomías might recall traditional
anthropological approaches that viewed the cargo system as central to the
definition and preservation of indigenousness, what I want to suggest here
is somewhat distinct. In the case of Tepetlaoxtoc, it would not really be
accurate to say that cargos are a structure that protects the community
from outside influence. Rather, they constitute an example of city people's
arrogance and foolishness because city people think that the mayordomía
is about putting on the fiesta when it is really about motivating others' participation. This kind of negative perception of city people reflects the fact
that villagers fail to see city people as an other because for them the other
is an interdependent subject and not an object, such as "a different way of
doing things." This local understanding of otherness has little to do with
what we usually think of as ethnicity, and thus the concept of ethnicity is
not particularly useful for understanding how residents of highland villages
conceptualize themselves and their relationships to others.

I return here to the question of the cargo system because it has occupied
a key role in the manner in which anthropologists have conceptualized the
distinction between indigenous culture and modernity and because, conveniently, Tepetlaoxtoc's residents refer to the example of cargos when they
are talking about the contrast between themselves and city people. Recall
that according to standard anthropological approaches, mayordomos are
the producers of culture in the form of the fiesta, but also, indirectly, they
act as producers of social structure, because the backbone of this structure
is imagined to be the cargo system of which the mayordomías are a central
part. This internal social structure also defines community boundaries.

Those who participate are part of the community, and those who do not are not. By obliging people to participate or by making it worth their while to do so, elders or leaders influence how community members spend their money, directing their spending toward community and away from the individualistic interests of the outside world. The fiestas and mayordomías are thus seen not only as the community's culture, social structure, or tradition but also as what keeps the modern world at bay. Resistance to modernization and the reproduction of indigenous ethnicity are equivalent to the preservation of the cargo system.

Apparently, people who move from the city to Tepetlaoxtoc as well as people from Tepetlaoxtoc who have spent all or most of their lives in the city before moving back understand the fiestas in a manner analogous to anthropologists. As if they had read ethnographies to prepare themselves for village life, when these people take on a mayordomía, they tend to try to pay for and put on the fiesta by themselves. Of course, they would not have to read an ethnography to think in this manner. The experience of life in the city is enough. They think they are acting in a morally correct manner because they are contributing to the community; they are, in their terms, being socially productive by producing things such as fiestas, community, and sociality.

For the people of Tepetlaoxtoc, meanwhile, the fiestas and mayordomías are about something quite distinct from reproducing culture and social structure or even the fiesta itself. While the fiesta as finished product is a minor concern, the truly important thing about the fiesta is that it is done "entre todos." Also, that people put on the fiesta "con gusto" rather than "con mala gana" is considered important by both villagers and the saint: as we have seen, the saint punishes actions done with mala gana. So what really matters is not so much the fiesta itself but how it is put on.

As demonstrated in chapter 3, putting on the fiesta entre todos and acting con gusto involve the production of active subjects. This kind of production can be seen clearly in the practices surrounding the mayordomía. The mayordomo's principal and most challenging task is to get others to participate. To accomplish this he goes from door to door asking people to *cooperar* by contributing cash. But this is not simply a question of walking around and collecting the money. Rather, he must motivate and convince people to cooperate. Thus the mayordomo produces not just a thing—the fiesta or cooperaciones—but, more importantly, action and subjectivities. When people talk about "hacer la fiesta entre todos," the key point is not to create a "todos," or in other words, the community, but rather to produce "el hacer," the doing, among as many people as possible.

While anthropologists and other urbanites have tended to dismiss the mayordomo's efforts aimed at getting others involved as simply one possible means for achieving what really matters—the fiesta or collective life—villagers see these efforts as essential. When people from Tepetlaoxtoc observe city people in the role of mayordomo, they are expecting these individuals to act as producers of subjects, not of things such as tradition or fiestas. So when they see that the city people do little to produce subjects and instead try to put the fiesta on by themselves, residents say that these mayordomos are *presumidos* (arrogant) because they act as if they do not need anyone else. This arrogance in turn is said to lightly veil a deeper ignorance or foolishness regarding how the world really works, since, in fact, people do need each other to be able to act as subjects. Whereas in the city, the independence demonstrated by these mayordomos in acting for the good of the collective would usually be commended, villagers completely miss these good intentions because they only notice the lack of production of active subjectivities and the foolishness of someone who sees this as unnecessary.

Representations of City People

One can hear villagers refer to city people as individualistic or arrogant fools in reference not just to fiestas but to other areas of life as well. For example, villagers sometimes note that city people are quite limited and inept when it comes to work because they can only do one thing—and this thing is usually business related—and cannot even perform simple tasks such as fixing things around the house. On other occasions, villagers state that city people are drug addicts and criminals, which upon further questioning seems to be a manner of saying that even if they are not all really addicts and criminals, they do not know how to live in a community. That is, since they are selfish and individualistic, they would have no problem stealing from others or wasting all of their time and money on themselves in the form of a drug addiction. *Drug addict* and *criminal* are metonyms that stand not so much for deviance as for something like being lost in individualism, like being arrogant or "acting big," and having wandered off life's correct path of interdependence.

The fact that villagers often see city people as arrogant fools is something that I believe needs to be taken seriously—not in the sense that city people really are foolish (although this may be the case for some of us) but rather because it suggests a wholly different notion of otherness than the one we usually imagine through concepts of cultural difference and ethnicity.

Although not frequently noted by ethnographers—who in most cases have paid little attention to how indigenous people see us—there is some other evidence of similar attitudes among indigenous peoples in the Americas. For example, Johannes Neurath (2008) states that the Huicholes consider "mestizos" to be "socially underdeveloped" because they "do not know or do not follow the law of reciprocity" (2008:35; my translation). Similarly, Gossen (1974) notes that residents of Chamula in highland Chiapas see themselves as occupying the center of the moral universe, leading the rest of it toward proper social behavior. Traveling away from the village is like going back in time to times and places of progressively more antisocial behavior. The manner in which Tepetlaoxtoc's residents represent people from the city particularly resonates with the portraits of "Whitemen" that Keith Basso (1979) found among Western Apaches. He notes that for Western Apaches "Whitemen lack modesty and humility, a characteristic that causes them to adopt an attitude of imperiousness and condescension when dealing with other people" (1979:58). Again like my informants, Western Apaches attribute this attitude among Anglo-Americans to the fact that they are "gross incompetents in the conduct of social relations" (1979:48). This incompetence is not simply attributable to cultural variation: "[T]he Anglo-American version is not only different but also seriously defective" (1979:56). Basso concludes, "To be sure, Whitemen have stolen land, violated treaties, and on numerous other fronts, treated Indians with a brutal lack of awareness and concern. But these are not the messages communicated by Western Apache jokers. Their sights are trained on *something more basic*, and that is making sense of how Anglo-Americans conduct themselves in the presence of Indian people. Here too, the Whitemen are frequently found guilty of incompetence and gross neglect" (1979:81–82; my emphasis). This kind of reaction to "Whitemen" and city people, seeing them as foolish and incompetent, suggests that Western Apaches and Tepetlaoxtoc villagers cannot quite make sense of Anglos and city people, respectively. I believe that they cannot make sense of such individuals because they have trouble seeing or grasping an Anglo-American or a city person as "an other."

To explain what I mean here, I need to set up a contrast between our (as anthropologists) own and their manner of seeing or conceiving of an other. Our method of seeing an other is to find or, better said, invent their culture, so that we have an object to see and to grasp. Or, as Viveiros de Castro puts it in his comparison between Western and Amerindian ontologies, "Objectification is the name of our game; what is not objectified remains unreal and abstract. The form of the other is *the thing*" (2004:468; emphasis in original). Most of our theories of cultural variation and ethnicity assume this to be a universal: others (including others' others) are those who live their lives differently or do things differently.

People in Tepetlaoxtoc sometimes make statements that could be interpreted to mean that they see the other in this manner: "La gente de la ciudad tiene otras costumbres" ("City people have other customs"). However, I believe that this is a nice way of saying that city people are bad mannered, since the word *costumbres* in Spanish can mean manners as well as customs.[3] What I really think happens in Tepetlaoxtoc is that people have trouble grasping city people as an other because for them the other is not an object, such as an ethnic group with a culture, but rather a subject. To cite Viveiros de Castro again, "Amerindian shamanism is guided by the opposite ideal. To know is to personify, to take on the point of view of that which must be known. Shamanic knowledge aims at something that is a someone—another subject. The form of the other is *the person*" (2004; emphasis in original). To think of otherness in Tepetlaoxtoc in a similar manner would be helpful. For people there to see or to "know," in Viveiros de Castro's terms, an other, this other must take the form of a subject or, more accurately for the case at hand, of a person ready to be subjectified and to subjectify and to enter a relation of interdependence. This interest in the production of active subjectivity and in interdependence is what people in Tepetlaoxtoc expect to encounter in people from the city, and when they fail to find it, since city people are concerned with producing or finding objects and not subjects, they end up seeing not a different kind of other but rather an absence, which they describe as foolishness or incompetence.

Anthropologists and other modern urbanites have usually imagined that the people we categorize as indigenous Mexicans view us as an other in basically the same manner that we view them: as a different ethnic group with a different culture. However, what I suggest here is that they see us in quite a different way because what draws their attention to an other is his production of subjects, not his production of objects such as culture. Thus, for them, what really matters about an other is not his difference but that he acts on or is acted on by them. This other is not a lifeless and distant thing but rather a live and interconnected person. This implies, I believe, that rural highland Mexicans are as unconcerned with what we think of as ethnicity as anthropologists usually are with the production of active subjects. If they are interested at all in what we think of as our "culture," it interests them not in and of itself but rather as a different means to the same end of producing and being produced as subjects.

Our usual imposition of our own ideas of ethnicity on people in highland communities is not just a theoretical problem but a practical one as well. Concepts such as multiculturalism and interculturalism, for example, which currently guide state policy regarding ethnicity (re indigenous people) in Mexico, are based on this universalizing notion of the other: otherness as an object, as something external from the person-as-subject and inert, or, more specifically, as a different culture. Such policies emerge from a desire to free so-called indigenous people from external impositions by opening state and society to other manners of understanding the world and living in it. In practice, however, they involve the imposition of a modern, Western notion of otherness based on the supposition that the differences among ethnic groups are to be found in the realm of culture or, in other words, in the realm of the things the group members have collectively produced. Such policies are especially pernicious because they not only perpetuate external impositions but also deceive us into thinking that we have solved the problem of diversity.

One consequence of this imposition is that so-called indigenous people must suppress practices that modern, Western actors do not consider "cultural," because they impinge on the modern, Western notion of nature. Thus, for example, they must hide the fact that their children begin to work and contribute to the family economy at a young age, since this is seen to be an abuse of children's natural condition of fragility and dependence. They must do so even though the fact that their sons and daughters work is, in reality, a reflection of the fact that they do not share our notion of family as a site for the production of sociality and culture in children. Rather, they view children as fully social and as interdependent participants in the production of active subjectivities. Another consequence of this imposition of multicultural policy is that it puts so-called indigenous people in a position from which they must *create* a culture for themselves in order to be recognized as an other and gain access to the state's programs and benefits. I suspect that the recent emergence of *usos y costumbres* (uses and customs) and *derecho consuetudinario* (consuetudinary law) in many communities throughout highland Mexico involves an act of creation more than one of revelation as residents attempt to fulfill the state's requirements for obtaining a modicum of political autonomy.

Modernity as Object versus Modernity as Conduit

Our interest in the production of things leads us to another questionable conclusion in our research: that the presence in villages of things we associate with traditional culture's antithesis, modernity, implies a process of modernization, by which we mean a process of change at the social level, usually seen as equivalent to progress. If ethnicity is about difference and culture, modernization is about heading toward a universal goal: the urban, the global, or the modern. So while culture and modernity are opposites in this sense, they are the same in another: both have to do with the production of things. Ethnicity is supposedly about the reproduction of traditional culture in the form of things such as fiestas, and modernization is supposedly about the production of things such as technology, education, science, and so forth. Georg Simmel's reflection on modern culture helps to clarify what I mean by this understanding of modernization as the production of things:

> [T]he development of modern culture is characterized by the preponderance of what one may call the "objective spirit" over the "subjective spirit." . . . If, for instance, we view the immense culture which for the last hundred years has been embodied in things and in knowledge, in institutions and in comforts, and if we compare all this with the cultural progress of the individual during the same period — at least in high status groups — a frightful disproportion in growth between the two becomes evident. Indeed, at some points we notice a retrogression in the culture of the individual with reference to spirituality, delicacy, and idealism. This discrepancy results essentially from the growing division of labour. For the division of labour demands from the individual an ever more one-sided accomplishment, and the greatest advance in a one-sided pursuit only too frequently means dearth to the personality of the individual. (2000:183–84)[4]

I suggest here that people in Tepetlaoxtoc approach modern culture and progress in a different manner. They see the things that constitute modernity not as ends in themselves but as means for improving upon the person. In other words, modernity is conceived of as a kind of conduit that allows for a different way of acting on and being acted on by others.

Progress Is Not Equivalent to Modernization

Villagers have a real interest in the modern/urban world, but for reasons that differ from what we usually understand as modernization. Even on a casual visit to the Texcoco region, and before coming across anything to do with fiestas, one would unavoidably observe characteristics of what we usually think of as the modern world: schools, technology (concrete structures, paved roads, piped water, electricity, etc.), businesses, industry, and even self-expression through consumption, as in the case of urban youth cultures. This apparent "modernization," combined with a lack of a structured civil-religious hierarchy, would be sufficient, I imagine, for anthropologists accustomed to the kind of "real" indigenous communities that we have usually studied to say that the region's villages have been completely modernized (see Encarnación Ruiz 2004). However, although the region's residents consider most of these modern adaptations to be important, at least much of the time, we should not confuse this interest in aspects of the modern world with a desire for modernization with its universal goals. Villagers do have a real interest in aspects of the modern/ urban world, but this is because those things serve local ends. Villagers are not simply interested in the things in and of themselves, as if possessing such things would solve their problems, and these things themselves do not constitute what villagers see as progress. This does not mean that the region's residents are indifferent to the specific qualities of local and modern things: some are sought and preserved while others are avoided. Generally speaking, I believe that villagers cherish things that facilitate interdependence and active subjectivity and reject those that hinder them. Fiestas are valued because they encourage the production of active subjectivity among people and between people and saints. Capitalist industry is viewed suspiciously because it can do the opposite, although it is often adopted as a necessary evil (see below). Being incorporated into the urban sprawl is also avoided for the threat this would posit to local values. In what follows, I provide more examples of how the region's residents selectively approach the incorporation of modernity and the defense of local practices.

A closer look at the piped water systems and schools, for example, shows that villagers try very hard to maintain control of such modern technologies and to prevent them from falling into government or private hands. This control allows the region's residents to take certain aspects of the modern and to leave others, such as when they accept the convenience and health benefits of piped water but resist its conversion into a "national" resource or a commodity. Villagers throughout the region see the water as belonging to the community because it is extracted from below the community's territory, and they see the system of pumps and pipes used to distribute it as belonging to the community because they or their ancestors built it. This position contradicts Mexican national law, which states that all underground resources including water are the property of the nation. In Tepetlaoxtoc, the elected members of the water committee occupy an office in the municipal government building, but they are quick to explain that they are completely independent from the municipal government. They insist that this arrangement is better since they can be sure that the fees people pay for their water will be used to run and maintain the system, whereas the government or a private provider would channel away at least part of what they pay.[5]

In the case of public schools, residents throughout the region, in contrast to parents in most of urban Mexico, form committees and participate actively in the schools' running and upkeep. They even go against national law by charging students' families additional fees to fund maintenance and improvements. Even the priesthood and thus the Catholic Church are only partially accepted by villagers. People recognize the priest's role in conducting masses or other rituals, which they consider essential to relations between humans, the saints, and God, but they are capable of ignoring or even expelling a priest who tries to make significant changes in local religious practices.

In his research on youth gangs in the village of San Jerónimo Amanalco, in Texcoco's sierra, Guillermo Torres demonstrates another example of this measured interest in the modern world (personal communication).[6] At first glance, one might think that a large percentage of the young men in the village are rebelling against local culture and adopting urban-modern ways in its place. They spend much of their free time with groups of other young men they refer to as *bandas* (gangs). The bandas carry the names of different urban youth subculture groups, usually linked to musical styles—such as "los Ska," "los Punks," and "los Metaleros"—and their members use the corresponding clothes and hairstyles. Each gang has its enemies and allies, and rumbles sometimes occur at dances held during fiestas. However, upon closer examination, according to Torres, these young men appear to be employing these urban styles to give a new twist to older practices. Gang membership is based principally on patrilineal kinship ties: members are cousins related through their fathers who have settled close together on land inherited from the gang members' grandfathers (see also Velásquez Velásquez 2007). Older generations in San Jerónimo grouped together in a similar manner, although they did not refer to themselves as bandas, and sometimes fought neighboring groups. San Jerónimo's gangs demonstrate concordance with local practices in another way as well. Each has its own patron saint, and they organize a fiesta in the saint's honor, acting as mayordomos, collecting cooperaciones, and getting others to participate in a manner analogous to how such celebrations are conducted at the barrio or village level. My point in discussing this example is not to claim that these young people are interested in reproducing traditional practices; as I argue above, this is not a primary concern when it comes to fiestas. Rather, I believe that the example suggests that young men are interested in new things such as urban youth styles—which are useful for distinguishing themselves from previous generations and from other peer groups—but, at the same time, they continue to share local interests in interdependence, and they have no overall goal of modernization or urbanization.

Aki Kuromiya (2006, 2010) in her study of Santo Tomás Apipilhuasco, another village in the Tepetlaoxtoc Municipality, found that residents are quite interested in what they call *progeso* (progress) or *salir adelante* (to move forward) but that they avoid the modern world's tendency to conflate progress or betterment with the modern or the urban. In the context of the village, progress refers to anything that increases comfort (*comodidad*) and may include modern technology such as cars and medicine. However, villagers also quickly reject modern technology that they see as unfavorable or threatening to their well-being, and they have no problem referring to what we would usually call traditional practices such as community self-government or the fiestas for patron saints as "progress" if these practices are seen to lead to greater well-being. Kuromiya (2006) provides, through a description of a debate among villagers over the widening of the highway that runs through the village, an example of how progress and betterment mean becoming more urban or modern only in limited ways. This apparently "modernizing" project was hailed by some as progress, while others opposed it. The interesting thing about the opposition was that it was also framed in terms of "moving forward" and not in terms of tradition and the preservation of tradition. The people living close to the highway simply saw its widening as something that would decrease rather than increase their comfort and well-being. These are the terms in which the debate was framed within the village; however, a discourse on the preservation of traditional culture would be used by residents to try to get their way in an urban context, where opposition to widening a highway is not usually understood as progress.

Returning to my own research in Tepetlaoxtoc, I was once witness to a discussion between two young men at a fiesta over how villagers should spend their money for the good of the community. One of them argued that instead of "burning" all of their money on fireworks, they should put it toward building a hospital. The other insisted that it was better for them to spend the money on "el patrón" (the boss, referring to St. Sebastián), implying that the saint's wrath would cause more problems than a hospital could possibly solve. He also added that when you give money for the fiesta you know where it will end up, referring to the fact that the saint will punish anyone who steals from him but that public works projects, especially those that are outside of villagers' control, are a good opportunity for corruption and graft. Most people listening seemed to agree with the latter argument, which was phrased just as much as the former in terms of "well-being." This example of the saint shows how well-being is really another way of talking about the production of subjectivity in an other: the villagers cause the saint to act and the latter, in turn, acts on the former.

James Maffie, a specialist in prehispanic Nahua philosophy, offers a comparison between modern Western and prehispanic Nahua epistemologies that helps to explain this more open or situational understanding of progress. He posits that in contrast to our universalistic goals, achieved through an epistemology concerned with absolute truths, "Nahua epistemology does not pursue goals such as truth for its own sake, accurate representation, empirical adequacy or manipulation and control; nor is it motivated by questions such as 'What is the (semantic) truth about nature?' or 'How can we master and bend the course of nature to our will?' As we've seen, *tlamatiliztli* [wisdom, knowledge] is performative, not discursive; creative and participatory, not passive or theoretical; concrete, not abstract; a 'knowing how,' not a 'knowing that'" (2003:78). One of the goals of this "knowing how" resonates with the concern with progress and comfort described by Kuromiya. Maffie states that tlamatiliztli "consists of the practical ability to conduct one's affairs in such a way as to attain some measure of equilibrium and purity—and hence some measure of well-being—in one's personal, domestic, social and natural environment" (2003:76). Jorge Klor de Alva makes a similar observation regarding the colonial period when he states that "unacculturated Nahua religiosity, in contrast to the Christian focus on salvation, was fundamentally apotropaic, that is, centered on averting evil through appropriate observances. Except to those few with a penchant for abstract thought, the misfortunes the Nahuas sought to avoid were very mundane: sickness, drought, hail, hunger, pests, poverty, sterility, and the many other calamities that attend bad luck" (1997:183). In other words, well-being is defined situationally and personally and not by anything allegedly universal such as the modern or the urban. Furthermore, knowledge is not part of culture, that is, a thing. Rather, it is situated in the person as performance, participation, conduct, or know-how. This version of progress is also interdependent because it is both a producer of and a product of such well-being in others: "The Nahua universe was a 'participatory universe' characterized by a 'relationship of compelling mutuality' or 'interdependence' between humans and universe" (Maffie 2003:76). In other words, we are talking about a goal that is constituted in action and is continuously causing and being caused by the action of others. We could say this goal is social in the sense that it is produced through interaction among different humans and other beings, but it is not social in the sense that we usually think of progress as being social, that is, as a thing or things that people produce, which then exist in a social realm beyond and external to persons.

Modernization as Conduit

Pitarch's (2003b) description of religious conversions in contemporary Chiapas suggests that the incorporation of European culture into indigenous life also occurs within the person rather than at the level of society. Converts are not looking for an absolute "truth" in these new religions. Rather, their concern is the practical question of how well the religion works to cure and prevent illness (2003b:69). Furthermore, conversion and its power to cure are imagined not as a question of faith or belief but in terms of how new practices enact bodily transformations. These bodily states, in turn, have an effect on people's souls, who were the ones causing the illness in the first place. Rather than being permanent, these bodily states are possibilities—actions, I might add—that can be accumulated and employed again in the future. People try out different religions to learn and appropriate the bodily states they offer—hence the multiple and frequent conversions (2003b:69). Once again, we see that change, or the incorporation of the new, including that which comes from the outside or the modern world, does not occur at the level of the "social" or the "cultural." It occurs at the level of persons, exists as action or subjectivity, and achieves well-being through interaction with others.

Marie-Noëlle Chamoux (1992) gives another helpful example of this particular manner of incorporating the "new" in her work on learning among contemporary Nahuas in the sierra region of the state of Puebla. She found that most learning involves a process of careful observation over an extended period. Teachers do not objectify knowledge in explanations or simulations—they teach by doing the real thing. And students go right from their period of observation to doing, without an intermediary period of trial and error or practice. Here, I would add that what is being learned—the "new"—is not an object but rather active subjectivity itself. Chamoux notes that this kind of teaching is not remunerated, for the learning process has no value in and of itself but is a means to an end. I would say that whereas we see "education" and "knowledge" as being valuable human products, that which has value for rural highland Mexicans is productive action. And further, the value of productive action is apparent not in the products but only in their use: "The proof of success is the utilization of the object, even if it is imperfect. The achievements are manifested in the fact that the product created by the apprentice is converted into use value *within the family*, or better still, when it becomes possible to turn it into exchange value by selling it in the market" (Chamoux 1992; my emphasis). I would add that the cash obtained from the sale of the object must also be directed toward the family for it to embody the value of the productive action. In other words, productive action is valuable only when it is transformed into ayuda. The process does not end with well-being and comfort, which do not attain their potential in and of themselves—well-being and comfort must be passed on to others as ayuda, thereby provoking and producing further action. Therefore, returning to the question of the incorporation of the new, we can say that learning a new work activity gives a particular shape to subjectivity or action, but the shape alone is insufficient to give action its value; rather, an action is truly valued as productive only when it produces subjectivity in others.

I think that people in Tepetlaoxtoc and other villages in the region incorporate the new in a manner similar to those described by Pitarch and Chamoux. In other words, what we would describe as modernization is for them a change, or really an addition, at the level of the person. As I describe above, villagers talk about city people who come to the village as either drug addicts and criminals or as presumidos who think they are superior and do not need anyone else. We find the same kind of reaction if we ask villagers their opinions of what city people are like in the city itself. However, there is also an idea that the city and its residents have something important to offer to villagers. The city offers job opportunities and money to be made, but perhaps more importantly, villagers talk about the city as a place where one can learn how to do business from city people. This means learning how to be sharp and quick, or to *moverse* (to position oneself to take advantage of opportunities and social relations), and how to take on different hierarchical roles in businesses. In a similar vein, Neurath observes that among the Huicholes, "[t]he cult of mestizo gods permits the appropriation of the enemies' 'dark powers' to triumph in the mestizos' capitalist world, but it also permits the development of an individual artistic creativity" (2008:37). However, this respect for city people's business know-how in Tepetlaoxtoc does not change villagers' overall opinion of them as inept, arrogant, and somewhat of a puzzle. It seems to surprise villagers that city people could be so good at one thing and so incapable when it comes to nearly everything else, including social life and what are seen as basic skills such as building and fixing a house. It also surprises villagers that despite their ineptitude, city people are still arrogant and base this feeling of superiority on something as insignificant as material possessions.

Conversely, it surprises us, as anthropologists, that *campesinos* frequently have multiple occupations. We usually attribute this to their ingenious survival skills under difficult circumstances. But I think it probably has at least as much to do with a manner of being in the world in which the new is incorporated at the level of the person, giving new shapes to subjectivity. In our modern world, with our progress, specialization, and division of labor, there are always more kinds of jobs that different people can hold, a kind of change that is considered "social" or "cultural." Among Tepetlaoxtoc's villagers, we could say that this kind of change, this specialization in economic activities, occurs at the level of the person, because specific people—not society—are the ones who accumulate more occupations.

As discussed in chapter 2, villagers are quite familiar with life in the city. Many villagers worked in unionized factory or government jobs before neoliberal reforms led to the elimination of many of these positions in the 1980s and 1990s. After losing their jobs many of these villagers returned to Tepetlaoxtoc, where they took up what would seem to be very distinct activities such as construction work, raising cattle, and clothes "assembly" (*maquila*). But even if the technical skills learned in the city were not of use in these new activities,[7] there are cases in which what they learned in a business sense and in particular the social roles played in urban economic activities are seen as quite useful. As we have seen from descriptions of the mayordomías and fiestas, villagers feel that it is important that when they do things together they should interact as equals and as subjects. This, in fact, is part of what makes putting on a fiesta such a challenge: if the mayordomo could simply tell people what to do, it would be easy. In contrast, villagers realize that running most businesses, even small ones, cannot work by doing things together in the same way that they do things together in the fiestas. Rather, for most businesses to function, people need to occupy different positions in a hierarchy, and they need to be like objects sometimes, following others' orders.[8] This is a way of being that must be learned from city people to do business. When residents bring this back to the village with them, it is supposed to be just a temporary way of being while they are doing business. It is not supposed to replace their usual egalitarian relations among subjects.

For example, Federico from Tepetlaoxtoc, a man in his early fifties, connects his recent success in the village as a contractor for construction

Figure 5.1 A small corral for "cattle fattening," a business enterprise taken up by many villagers after losing jobs in Mexico City because of economic crises and neoliberal budget cuts of the 1980s and 1990s. The owner has, at least for the moment, given up this potentially lucrative but risky venture. Tepetlaoxtoc, 2011.

work to the fact that previously, in the city, he had worked his way up in a large company from vacation substitute to district sales manager. He emphasizes that he learned not only how to be a boss in the city but how to take on the role of employee as well. He explained that because of his varied experience in the city, when he cannot find work as a contractor he is able to take on any one of the three lower positions in the construction industry: *maestro* (foreman), *albañil* (worker), or even the lowly post of *ayudante* or *chalán* (worker's assistant). And while I would not deny that his position as frequent contractor gives Federico at least temporary power over fellow villagers, I have seen him drink and play soccer with these same people in a manner that does not suggest hierarchy. Furthermore, if one of his employees lands a contract, the roles might be switched around. In the village, these roles are supposed to be seen as temporary, and they do not define the person in a permanent sense. Even if someone has learned in the city how to be a boss, he will have trouble with his employees in the village if he is presumido and acts superior to others and as if he does not need them.

Minerva López Millán (2008), in her study of the neighboring village of Santa Catarina del Monte, where many residents work as florists, finds that they consider spending time working and living in the city as essential if one wants to return to the village and work successfully as a florist. Aspiring florists, even if they have fathers, uncles, or older brothers who work as florists in the village, go to work in a business in the city, starting out on the lowest rung and even sleeping in the store or stand. Eventually they will move up into higher positions in the florist hierarchy, but always working under an owner who is a "city person." During this time they will learn the technical aspects of being a florist, such as doing arrangements, but this is something they could have learned in the village. What they really go to the city to learn is how to occupy different positions in a business hierarchy. When they return to the village they will do so as "florists," regardless of the last position they held in the city, and no one works for anyone else in a permanent sense as in the city. However, when someone finds work (for example, doing arrangements for a fiesta), he will usually have to hire others to work for him. In these temporary situations, the florists take on the different roles learned in the city, giving or taking orders, while at the same time teasing or joking about the hierarchy, which contradicts the notion that they are all equal as florists in the village.

We could say once again that this kind of learning does not imply anything like cultural change or modernization at the level of the village. Each would-be florist must go to the city to learn and incorporate the new way of being, because only in the city is there opportunity for prolonged observation and experience of the business hierarchy. This example of the florists, along with the others mentioned here, suggests that what we might usually think of as a modernization of the village economy really occurs at the level of the person where conduits for subjectivities are incorporated. Thus, much of the region's apparent modernization must be understood not in terms of the production or borrowing of modern things but rather as the accumulation of urban or modern shapes or conduits for subjectivities. As we have already seen (see chapter 4), López Millán (2008) then goes on to show that for villagers these modern conduits and the products and profits derived from them are valued, but as means to another end. Real value, or what she refers to as "person-value," is produced when people give their products and profits to others, thereby demonstrating their subjectivity and causing it subsequently in others.

The Flourishing of Interdependence in Tepetlaoxtoc and Contemporary Global Capitalism

This description of how people from Tepetlaoxtoc and the region as a whole interact with the urban-modern world and how they practice change probably makes it sound as if they had complete control over their own destinies even in relation to the state and global capitalism. Of course this is not the case. Rather, what I describe here is contingent upon circumstances specific to the time and place. Generally speaking, we could say that over the past thirty or so years, people in the region have had access to the urban-modern world while being basically left alone to take it or leave it as they please. One reason why they are in this position in relation to the urban-modern is that unlike more accessible regions in the Valley of Mexico that were flooded with urban growth during the city's moment of explosive growth between about 1950 and 1980, the partial barrier of the dry lakebed slowed or delayed that growth in the Texcoco region. Although the region has received a fair number of immigrants looking for inexpensive housing within commuting distance from Mexico City, especially since the highway crossing the dry lakebed was opened in 1994, the number of such immigrants does not compare with the quantity of people who have settled in areas such as Chalco and Ecatepec. This flood of migrants to these other areas, even while many came from rural highland villages themselves, meant an imposition of modern-urban ways of being and relating socially. In contrast, villagers in the Texcoco region are still able to impose their own ways of living on an immigrant minority.

Aside from the limited urban migration to the region, there is another explanation as to why the region has been spared the full effects of urban influence. As noted in chapter 2, the region has remained deurbanized in the sense that it lacks many public and private services as well as certain economic activities, due to the fact that Mexico City's proximity obviates the need to repeat these services and activities in the region (see Bonfil Batalla 1973). Thus, in contrast to Redfield's (1970 [1941]) theory that urbanization is brought about by proximity to urban centers, small cities that are close to large ones tend to remain deurbanized in the sense of not becoming important political and economic centers. To give an example of this, it is notable that the only public university in the region is an agricultural school that attracts few students from this largely nonagricultural area.[9] Most of the region's residents who aspire to a university education hope to attend one of the public universities in Mexico City or Toluca. People in the region hardly consider this lack of universities a benefit, but it is both an indicator and a cause of the region's being "off the map" of urban development. This deurbanization due to proximity to a major urban center thus constitutes an important factor in keeping to a minimum the imposition of aspects of the urban-modern on the region's residents.

Of course, some urban services require proximity to the city without being right in it, which is probably why the region's residents have been threatened with the construction of an international airport and a garbage dump in recent years.[10] These examples are useful for demonstrating the limits of the region's freedom from imposed urbanization and the fragility of people's control over their lives. I use the word *threatened* in the earlier sentence because most residents saw these two projects as unwelcome impositions that would imply a loss of control over their resources and lives in general. The garbage dump, which would have received wastes from a significant proportion of Mexico City's residents, was, in 2008, proposed for private lands just outside of the village of Tepetlaoxtoc. Residents organized and successfully opposed the project, claiming worries over the contamination of their water supply and the negative effects on tourism caused by the unsightly dump and its unpleasant odors.[11] As I state in chapter 2, the airport was seen as a serious threat to people throughout the region, in particular to the residents of San Salvador Atenco, on whose ejidal lands it was to be built. The success of the protests against these two impositions might seem to suggest that the region's residents really can control their destiny, but I think that what it really shows is that they recognize their vulnerability, and although they won a battle, it is undoubtedly not the end of the war, as few options exist for urban expansion and development near Mexico City. There even exists a new proposal to build an airport on federal lands a bit farther from the shore and the villages, and there is no indication that these new plans take the region's residents into account any more than the earlier one.

We could say that the garbage dump and the airport constituted major, external threats to the people in the region, but there also exist threats on a more local level. Rubén Lechuga Paredes (2004) in his study of social change in the village of Tlaltecahuacan describes a situation that contrasts sharply with nearby Atenco: villagers in Tlaltecahuacan seem to be losing a battle against outsiders who are buying up agricultural lands to build dwellings, workshops, and businesses. Lechuga Paredes attributes this, in part, to the fact that the village falls under the jurisdiction of a powerful, abusive, cacique-like municipal president. The fact that the village is not the municipal seat makes it particularly vulnerable, because municipal presidents often ignore the interests of other villages in favor of those of the seat. Lechuga Paredes recounts how this particular president accepts bribes from potential buyers of land and water in exchange for facilitating access to these resources and bypassing village leaders. He thereby helps to convert these resources into commodities with no concern for the effects of his actions on his constituents in Tlaltecahuacan. The example of Tlaltecahuacan demonstrates the need to recognize that even in the region at the present time, not all residents have the same level of control over the manner in which they live their lives.

Another example of how my description of life in the region is historically contingent has to do with the effects of neoliberal reforms during the 1980s and 1990s. As mentioned in chapter 2, Tepetlaoxtoc was somewhat of a ghost town in the 1960s and 1970s, as many villagers were drawn to the capital by employment opportunities attributable to the country's rapid economic growth during this period. A study of community and family life during this period may not have led to conclusions about a vibrant life involving interdependent action and the production of active subjects. Then, in the 1980s and 1990s, many of these villagers lost their jobs because of economic crises and neoliberal reforms. Often they returned to Tepetlaoxtoc, where they could live rent-free on inherited land, repopulating the village and giving new life to the fiestas and other practices. Thus, it could be said that we are dealing with a historical moment in which Tepetlaoxtoc's or the region's residents are basically left alone by the state and global capitalism because there is little direct interest in them as workers or as citizens. In the half century leading up to their incorporation into the rapidly industrializing urban workforce in the 1960s, this was not the case. As in many other parts of rural Mexico during this period, the government used schools to transform indigenous peasant villagers into Spanish-speaking modern Mexican citizens. And while the transformation might not have been as profound as the government imagined and the category "mestizo" suggests (failing to do away with interdependence, for example), this transformation was significant both to state strategy and to the local population. In contrast, the recent neoliberal governance strategy prefers not to deal with such an "excess" population at all, leaving them alone to fend for themselves, which is distinct from the other common neoliberal strategy, which involves transforming people into autonomous individuals. It is this recently repopulated community, ignored by current state political-economic strategy and sustained by a functioning but precarious regional economy, that I describe here.

Now I have swung the pendulum the other way, and perhaps it sounds as if the region's residents have had no control whatsoever over their destiny. To put things back in balance, I should add that many people saw the loss of jobs in the city as a blessing in disguise and as an opportunity to relive the community and familial practices of interdependence that they longed for while living in the city. Villagers told me that while they miss the stability and benefits of jobs in the city, living and working in the village has the advantage of leaving more time for these practices. They also noted that owning their own small business in the village, fattening cattle or doing maquila work, presents an opportunity to make a lot more money than they would ever have made in their jobs in the city. In reality, few small business owners have been that successful, but this fact does not stop most people from choosing to try their hand at business. People also state that they prefer to work at or near home with kin and friends rather than in the city with strangers. Jay Sokolovsky (2010) found that among young married couples who are doing maquila work at home, one of the benefits they claim is the opportunity to spend more time together. Frances Rothstein (2007) also sees villagers' agency in their establishment of small businesses close to home. She argues that among villagers in the neighboring state of Tlaxcala, local maquila workshops, where owners hire their own kin as workers, are a form of resistance against more abusive forms of capitalist exploitation outside the village (2007:137). I would add that it is precisely the weight of interdependence that mitigates abuse in these local workshops: people cannot take too seriously their hierarchical roles and the idea that owners control workers' actions. But the reverse is also true. Interdependence limits workers in the collective demands they can make on their kin employers. Rothstein notes that workers deal with this problem by changing jobs frequently, thereby allowing people to avoid confrontations that would necessarily result in one party imposing itself on the other (Rothstein 2007:91). In Tepetlaoxtoc, small business owners who are known to demonstrate their need for others through cooperation and participation in fiestas and other community activities have an advantage when it comes to attracting clients and workers. However, villagers also recognize that this recognition of interdependence complicates the ruthlessness and impersonality that are often needed to make capitalist enterprises a success (see Magazine 2010).

I would also like to suggest another explanation as to why people in the region, and perhaps in other parts of rural Mexico, are being largely left alone by the state and other agents of global capitalism, in the sense that there are no great efforts to modernize them. It may be the case that they are being left alone in this sense not because, or at least not only because, they are superfluous but because they are doing something that

Figure 5.2 "Garment worker sought. Urgent," a sign posted in the central plaza of Tepetlaoxtoc, 2011. The growth of the region's garment industry, centered in the village of Chiconcuac, has not displaced local emphasis on the production of active subjectivity.

fulfills some sort of need. I am thinking of capitalism's constant need for motivated workers and the current need in much of Mexico and the world for "flexible" workers willing to take temporary jobs. It is usually assumed that such needs must be fulfilled by creating such workers, often through the socialization of people and especially children into a particular sort of work culture. However, it would be extremely convenient and inexpensive for capitalism to find motivated, and in this case, flexible workers instead of having to create them. I believe that something like this may be what makes rural Mexicans attractive to employers within Mexico and in the United States (Magazine and Ramírez Sánchez 2007:69).

Figure 5.3 The juxtaposition of a corn field and a suburban-style house exemplifies villagers' accumulation of both rural and urban practices. Tepetlaoxtoc, 2011.

As I attempt to show in chapter 4, motivation to work in Tepetlaoxtoc and the region comes from other people—more specifically, from parents in the case of sons and daughters and from sons and daughters in the case of parents. In contrast, in the modern urban world, good workers are imagined as those who motivate themselves to work. This motivation, in turn, is seen as a combination of the individual's will and an ethic that the worker has internalized that links work to morality. Generally speaking, in the modern urban world, a good person is one who takes care of himself as well as others through what he earns working and who contributes to society by working. To look at this ethic in another way, there is an exchange that goes beyond payment for labor: people are motivated to work because they see it as what defines them and fulfills them as persons. Great efforts, mostly in formal education, are made to instill this work ethic in people, because "a 'stone-age economics'" is thought to prevail in its absence, "in which they only work to fulfill natural basic necessities" (Magazine and Ramírez Sánchez 2007:55). But even after these great efforts are made, the situation is still precarious, because certain jobs may not provide the self-definition and fulfillment that workers expect. Under neoliberalism and flexible capitalist accumulation, for example, many jobs are too fleeting to fulfill workers' expectations, making it difficult to keep them motivated. One solution has been to invest more effort into modifying the ethic, giving value to flexibility (see Martin 1994).

What I would like to suggest here is that people such as those from the Texcoco region whose motivation to work does not necessarily have to do with self-fulfillment in the workplace or with what they learned at school constitute another, cheaper solution. For these people, one of the main purposes of life is to provide ayuda to others. The motivation to fulfill this purpose does not have to be taught; rather, it is constantly created anew by one's family members through their provisions of ayuda. And while paid labor is in most cases necessary to complete this purpose because ayuda is frequently provided as cash, work is seen as a means to an end in such a way that people do not generally look to work for fulfillment. Thus, these workers have a constant source of motivation but at the same time approach their work with a certain amount of indifference: a nearly perfect solution for employers who want good, constant workers who will not be terribly upset to lose their jobs. Considering this fit between workers from rural Mexico and contemporary global capitalism, it should not surprise us too much that lately, the latter's agents are pretty much leaving the former alone rather than trying to modernize them.

SIX

Bridging the Gap

This book constitutes an attempt to suggest the benefits of a shift in our approach to the study of the lives of rural highland peoples in Mexico. Many of anthropology's usual topics and approaches in the region unavoidably derive from our own culturally and historically determined manner of being in and understanding the world and thus can distract from and even distort what is truly important to the people whose lives we study. I propose that one way to work toward correcting these distortions is through attention to local understandings of social practices, which we can then incorporate into anthropological thinking and approaches. This incorporation serves to increase our awareness of the cultural specificity and thus the limitations of not merely our theory but the assumptions that underlie our theory and to help us to eliminate this ethnocentrism from the conceptual tools we use to describe and understand the people we study. Thus, I see this work as part of a broader disciplinary effort (e.g., Strathern 1988; Viveiros de Castro 1998, 2004; Wagner 1981 [1975]) aimed at bridging the epistemological gap between our informants and data, on the one hand, and us and our work, on the other.

Ironically, in my attempt to bridge this gap I emphasize this dichotomy between the modern West and highland Mexico. But this dichotomy is implicitly present in most anthropological work, maintained and obscured through the distancing techniques of anthropological writing (Fabian 1983). The explicitness with which this dichotomy appears here is a consequence of my bringing both sides together on the same level, of putting them into a dialogue between equals. This conceptual exercise has, of course, meant distorting the matter and positing a homogenous and bounded modern West and highland Mexico. In reality, each is varied and changing, and together they are interconnected or even indistinguishable, as I attempt to show at moments in the text.

Specifically, I suggest that while we, as anthropologists, usually focus on the production of things such as culture, social structure, and community, our highland Mexican informants are more concerned with the production of active subjectivity and with interdependence, and therefore, we should shift our focus and our thinking to incorporate these local interests and understandings. In previous chapters I use the example of three classic topics—fiestas and cargos, family and kinship, and ethnicity and modernization—to demonstrate how we might go about this substitution. In the case of fiestas and cargos, I contrast anthropology's focus on the production of community and of status with my informants' concern with producing action in others, with living their interdependence, and with creating a literal togetherness constituted by parts of persons united through exchanges. It is not that fiestas and community do not matter, but they matter more as means to an end than as ends in themselves, which is how anthropology has generally understood them. I make a similar argument in relation to family and kinship, attempting to demonstrate that our usual approach to family as a site for social reproduction and survival has distracted us from a local concern with producing a literal togetherness—which does not necessarily imply sharing interests and goals—and action in others through exchanges of ayuda. Family members are indeed dedicated to producing material goods necessary for survival or even the accumulation of wealth, but these things would mean little if they were not part of an exchange of goods that produces people to act as sons, daughters, fathers, and mothers. In relation to ethnicity and modernization, I posit that our fixation on otherness as object and on continuity and change at the sociocultural level distorts our comprehension of our informants' understanding of otherness as subjectivity and their attempts to effect change at the level of the person. This awareness of our informants' understanding of otherness as subjectivity and of modernity as a conduit permits us to begin to imagine how local understandings and practices can coexist with global capitalism, national politics, and other sources of external influence. In other words, it helps us to conceptualize how the inhabitants of a village such as Tepetlaoxtoc can be so modern and urban and, at the same time, display a manner of being in and understanding the world that is clearly different from dominant modern-urban cultural forms. I should add that while I found these three topics to be useful to my task, they are simply examples and do not constitute the problem or the solution in and of themselves.

If I feel fairly secure in my position regarding the limitations of our usual approaches, I must admit that I am less sure when it comes to the alternative that I propose here: a focus on the production of active subjectivity and on interdependence. Thus, I wish to emphasize the suggestive nature of this proposal. I hope that my colleagues will contribute to or in some cases continue to contribute to this effort to formulate new and more-effective approaches to understanding the lives of highland Mexicans. I am sure that there are other ways of describing the same sort of sociocultural phenomena, some of which are undoubtedly more illustrative and accurate. I should add that by no means am I suggesting that any of these approaches, and surely not my own, rises above the kind of ethnocentric limitation noted above. Rather, such new approaches distance us from some of our assumptions only to embed our interpretations in others, thereby leaving plenty of work for a continuing critical anthropology.

And if I am somewhat insecure in my formulation for understanding social practices in Tepetlaoxtoc, I am even less confident regarding my proposal of its applicability to communities in other parts of highland Mexico. My doubt derives not only from this world region's significant sociocultural heterogeneity but also from the fact that Tepetlaoxtoc, with its proximity to Mexico City, its cash economy, and its Spanish monolinguism, is hardly typical of the kind of isolated, rural highland community usually studied by anthropologists. However, the similarities that I have come across in my colleagues' descriptions of other communities throughout this world region, and that I have frequently cited and drawn upon here, lead me to believe that the proposal does have broader relevance, even if I do not expect that researchers working in other communities will find practices and understandings identical to the ones I describe here. Thus, I hope that my proposal will be read not as a rigid formula but as an attempt to direct attention to certain local practices and understandings and their potential for contributing to a revision of our usual approaches and assumptions.

Finally, I would like to reiterate that this problem of the distortions caused by imposing our own understandings on others is not just theoretical. Rather, in Mexico as in other parts of the world, such understandings influence the formulation of public policy or, in more general terms, "governmentality" (Foucault 1991) and thus affect people's lives in concrete ways. Considering that such distorted understandings have concrete, negative effects on people's lives, we urgently need to work toward new conceptualizations of these lives as well as new formulations of otherness and of what we all have in common. More specifically, we need to move beyond the thing-oriented multiculturalism that currently occupies a dominant position in governmentality in Mexico and in many other places, toward a new, truly universal, conceptualization of Mexicanness or of humanity. This new conceptualization would not have to reflect an already existing human universality—if such a thing exists—but could attempt to formulate and create it. The highland Mexican conceptualization of other-as-subject might be a good place to start. It has the benefit of emphasizing sameness over difference; in addition, its focus on persons might help steer us away from the alienation and frenzied material production that the capitalist obsession with things has brought us.

Notes

Chapter 1. Introduction

1. By "we" I mean "sociocultural anthropologists," including myself.

2. I am using the term *production* to represent a whole category of similar terms such as *reproduction, creation,* and *appropriation.* I group these terms together because all of them concern human action and its ends. What I am really interested in here is not so much what precisely is implied by *production* versus, for example, *creation,* but rather what we imagine the principal ends of human action to be in different settings.

Chapter 2. The Texcoco Region and the Village of Tepetlaoxtoc

1. *Extensive production* refers to the cultivation of crops such as corn or wheat requiring more land and less labor, while *intensive production* refers to the cultivation of crops such as flowers or fruit requiring less land and more labor.

2. See Kyle 2008 for a complete and insightful description of a process of the dissolution of regional self-sufficiency in another part of Mexico.

3. One of the most significant reforms of the 1910 Revolution was the return of lands, seized by haciendas and plantations, to rural communities in the form of the *ejido.* The ejido system combines communal administration with individual usufruct rights and federal government oversight. The constitutional reform of 1992 permitted the sale of ejidal lands. However, the government practiced the privatization of ejidal lands in cases of urban expansion prior to the 1992 reform.

4. In 2008, the government announced a new plan to construct the airport on federal lands, closer to the center of the dry lakebed. Residents of Atenco continue to oppose its construction, arguing that it will negatively affect the area's ecosystem.

5. Atenco's residents were not as successful in this confrontation with authorities as in the case of the airport. When they closed the highway that passes by the village, police from the state of Mexico brutally attacked protesters, capturing many and sending them to prison.

6. I refer here to the image of the saint, although villagers refer to these images not as objects but as the saint him- or herself.

7. Even its power as political center has declined in recent years. Whereas previously nearly all of the municipal presidents came from the municipal seat, over the past twenty years the tendency has reversed and the majority have come from other villages—in particular, the villages of Jolalpan, a plains village, and Apipilhuasco, a sierra village, the second and third largest villages in the municipality in terms of population after the seat.

8. Pulque is an alcoholic beverage made from the maguey plant. Because it continues to ferment, it cannot be bottled and must be consumed fresh.

9. The only public university in the region is an agricultural school (Universidad Autónoma de Chapingo), and Mexico City is closer than the state capital, Toluca, where the state of Mexico's public university is located.

10. At the time of my research, the exchange rate was approximately ten pesos to the dollar.

11. Because of this success, Jolalpan could be said to have surpassed Tepetlaoxtoc as the municipality's economic center.

Chapter 3. "La fiesta se hace entre todos"

Author's note: An earlier version of this chapter was published under the title "'We All Put on the Fiesta Together': Interdependence and the Production of Active Subjectivity through Cargos in a Highland Mexican Village" in volume 16, no. 2 of the *Journal of Latin American and Caribbean Anthropology*, copyright 2011 by the American Anthropological Association.

1. Appadurai (1986) uses the term *gate-keeping* to refer to topics that dominate and guide anthropological work on a world region, such as descent in Africa or hierarchy in South Asia, and also impede or devalue attention to other topics.

2. My historical data come from oral sources; I lack information regarding how fiestas were organized prior to the Revolution. A ladderlike civil-religious hierarchy could have existed at some point in the village's history, but I see no reason to assume that it did.

3. The receipts usually have the saint's name, the year, and a picture of the saint on top. Just below that appears the mayordomo's name and the names of his three principal compañeros and then below that a list of the other compañeros. The mayordomo or compañero writes the person's name and the amount given on both the receipt and the stub, which he keeps.

4. Thinking of Pitarch's conceptualization of bodily transformations as a particularly important form of action among Tzeltales in Chiapas (Pitarch 2003b), I have to wonder whether in Tepetlaoxtoc alcohol is also seen to bring about participation through the transformation of bodies and perspectives.

5. Brandes notes something similar in Tzintzuntzan but without attributing much importance to it: "Generally, it is already known before selection who in the community is willing to accept such a charge; nonetheless, I have never heard of a person actually volunteering before being formally drafted" (1988:49).

6. To protect my informants' anonymity I refer to them using pseudonyms throughout the text.

7. Rodríguez Hernández finds that in the neighboring village of Chiconcuac, doing a cargo by oneself is likewise looked down on: "[T]he inhabitants of Chiconcuac

explain that one person alone cannot fill a cargo; even if he has a lot of money and can pay specialized services to serve and prepare the food, it is not considered correct, nor is it conceived that this can be a way of fulfilling the commitment 'como debe ser' ('as it should be')" (2008:137; my translation).

8. Antonio was originally from a small *ranchería* (homestead) near Tepetlaoxtoc and had moved there so that his children could attend school. The ranchería's patron saint was La Santísima Trinidad, and he explained his particular interest in this relatively minor fiesta in Tepetlaoxtoc over that of "el patrón," San Sebastián, in terms of his membership in this other community.

9. I have dealt elsewhere with this apparent contradiction among street children in Mexico City (Magazine 2003a).

10. This most basic form of firework consists of a small rocket attached to a long stick. A person holds the stick and lights the rocket, which after a second or two takes off into the sky and eventually explodes. There are some dangers involved, principally, that the rocket might explode without flying out of the person's hand; this possibility may then frighten the holder, who lets go of the stick too soon, causing it to leave his hand with less force and thus taking off sideways to possibly explode among bystanders.

11. This idea that drinking should not be done alone makes it almost impossible for men to refrain from drinking when other men around them start. Refraining from drinking in a social situation is always a struggle and requires ready excuses, such as the fact that one is taking medication or is *jurado* (sworn to have stopped drinking to the Virgin or a saint), and persistence.

12. This manner of talking about community possessions resonates with Monaghan's discussion of the Mixtec term *kua-io ta'a* in Nuyoo, Oaxaca, which means "of all of us relatives/friends/Nuyootecos" and can refer to tortillas pooled in the fiesta but also to the community's territory and to public buildings (Monaghan 1990:767).

13. The parish church is possibly an exception. While I would imagine that the villagers also consider it to be theirs, I think that they concede control over it to the priest. Although it is by far the biggest church in the village and is located next to the central plaza, its saint, Mary Magdalene, and thus the church itself, is relatively unimportant for the villagers.

Chapter 4. Ayuda Among and Within Families

1. In a similar vein, Taggart notes that "Nahuat in Huitzilan represent marriage by saying that a man and a woman 'work for each other' (motequipanoah)" (2007:99). While in my own research I focused more on intergenerational relations, I believe that much the same could be said about relations between husbands and wives, as Taggart's observation suggests.

2. This potential for confusion between the standard Spanish and the Mesoamerican understanding of *ayuda* became apparent to me after hearing a comment in response to a conference paper in which women's wage earning was referred to as "ayuda." The person making the comment stated that by using such terms, rural women were contributing to the undervaluation of their own labor. This comment makes sense if what we understand is that these women are "just helping their husbands out." For us, "help" is seen in a positive light because it implies selflessness, but it is also considered to be secondary or tangential because if there is "help" then there is also the "real"

work or "real" production to which the help is being added. However, among people in the Texcoco region, the effort implied by ayuda is not secondary but rather central to production—the production of subjects. A wife who gives ayuda is not demonstrating her weakness but rather doing something akin to exercising power in relation to her husband—not in the sense of controlling him but rather motivating him to act.

3. Mole is a dark-colored sauce made from ground-up chiles and spices. Barbacoa is mutton cooked slowly, usually in a hole dug in the ground. Carnitas refers to pork deep-fried in lard. Tlacoyos are oblong corn tortillas filled with a bean paste or other ingredients.

4. His fellow band members will agree, knowing that he will do the same when they want to give the same gift to their own family members.

5. See Robichaux (1997, 2005) for a general discussion of the development cycle of domestic groups in Mesoamerica.

6. I make this claim for the Texcoco region based on how people link togetherness and exchanges of ayuda. However, in Good Eshelman's work on Nahuas in the state of Guerrero, this extension of the person through exchanges is much more explicit: "From the local point of view, by working one transmits his *fuerza* [force] and, therefore, by receiving the benefits of someone else's work one receives his *fuerza*. Yet more interesting is the fact that for the Nahuas objects contain the *fuerza* of the persons that produce them" (Good Eshelman 2005:288).

Chapter 5. Problems with "Ethnicity" and "Modernization"

1. Other authors reject these possibilities of cultural continuity entirely. Friedlander (1975), for example, dismisses concerns with indigenous culture and with acculturation or resistance to acculturation, arguing that the residents of a village in the state of Morelos have nothing to tell us about this topic because their beliefs and practices are a product not of the prehispanic past but of the colonial and national periods. Her interest is in how villagers employ the category "indio" to classify themselves and each other in terms of poverty and backwardness. She also shows how indigenous culture and identity are enacted for political and economic purposes. As with the examples of cargos and family discussed above, questions of sociocultural difference, boundaries, and transformation are dropped without a critical examination of underlying theoretical assumptions. The problem, apparently, was not with our conceptualization of sociocultural difference and boundaries but that our obsession with them led us to neglect agency and, more specifically, to mistake political claims to indigenous culture with the real thing. And if this real thing, in the form of indigenous culture or social structure, could not be found, it was not because we had invented it to begin with but because after five hundred years of domination by European culture, it had, not surprisingly, all but disappeared.

2. This is inversely parallel to our reaction to practices among other groups of people such as bodily mutilation or scarification that are difficult for us to see as culture because they destroy, rather than control and build upon, "nature." Rather than recognizing these actions as "another way of doing things," we condemn them as an abomination of nature, and we see these people as using their natural ability to act for destructive instead of productive purposes. Such a person is not an other but an aspect of universal humanness gone awry.

3. I am indebted to David Robichaux for suggesting this interpretation in a personal communication.

4. Simmel's essay "The Metropolis and Mental Life" was originally published in 1903.

5. Ennis-McMillan (2001) describes a similar logic in a neighboring village.

6. Torres's research on this topic is currently unpublished.

7. The technical skills required for these new activities were likely acquired previous to their time working in the city. Villagers frequently mention having learned to do construction work or raise cattle as children before going to the city.

8. Interestingly, Bashkow, in his study of how people in a Melanesian community understand white people, notes something similar: "Orokaiva often complain that 'we all want to be boss,' whereas whitemen can obey one another and accept subordinate positions. Whitemen seem to be able to undertake group projects without jealousy and personal resentment, allowing their individual wills to be constrained within external structures" (Bashkow 2006:69).

9. The Universidad Autónoma de Chapingo is just to the south of the city of Texcoco.

10. This proximity has also led to the emergence of economic activities, such as clothes assembly and cattle fattening (see chapter 2), that require low-rent spaces that are close to the city and thus keep shipping costs down. Residents do not seem to view this emergence as a threat, probably because these activities provide work conveniently at home or close to home without obviously imposing other kinds of transformations.

11. There are a few weekend homes in the village owned by wealthy Mexico City residents and a few sites that attract some day visitors, including two sixteenth-century structures: a Dominican convent and fray Domingo de Betanzos' hermitary and chapel.

References

Aguirre Beltrán, Gonzalo
   1973 [1967]   Regiones de refugio: El desarrollo de la comunidad y el proceso
      dominical en mestizoamérica. Mexico City: SEP / INI.

Appadurai, Arjun
   1986   Theory in Anthropology: Center and Periphery. Comparative Studies in
      Society and History 28 (2): 356–67.

Arizpe, Lourdes
   1980   La migración por relevos y la reproducción social del campesinado. Mexico
      City: El Colegio de México.

Bartra, Roger
   1978   Estructura agraria y clases sociales en México. Mexico City: Editorial Era.

Bashkow, Ira
   2006   The Meaning of Whitemen: Race and Modernity in the Orokaiva Cultural
      World. Chicago: University of Chicago Press.

Basso, Keith H.
   1979   Portraits of "the Whiteman": Linguistic Play and Cultural Symbols among
      the Western Apache. Cambridge: Cambridge University Press.

Bonfil Batalla, Guillermo
   1973   Cholula: La ciudad sagrada en la era industrial. Mexico City: UNAM, IIH.

Brandes, Stanley
   1981   Cargo versus Cost Sharing in Mesoamerican Fiestas, with Special Refer-
      ences to Tzintzuntzan. Southwest Journal of Anthropology 37:209–25.
   1988   Power and Persuasion: Fiestas and Social Control in Rural Mexico. Philadel-
      phia: University of Pennsylvania Press.

Bricker, Victoria
   1973   Ritual Humor in Highland Chiapas. Austin: University of Texas Press.

Broda, Johanna
2001 La etnografía de la fiesta de Santa Cruz: Una perspectiva histórica. *In* Cosmovisión, ritual e identidad de los pueblos indígenas de México, edited by J. Broda and F. Báez-Jorge, 165–238. Mexico City: CONACULTA / Fondo de Cultura Económica.

Broda, Johanna, and Félix Báez-Jorge, eds.
2001 Cosmovisión, ritual e identidad de los pueblos indígenas de México. Mexico City: CONACULTA / Fondo de Cultura Económica.

Campos de García, Margarita
1973 Escuela y comunidad en Tepetlaoxtoc. Mexico City: SEP / SETENTAS.

Cancian, Frank
1965 Economics and Prestige in a Maya Community. Stanford: Stanford University Press.
1992 The Decline of Community in Zinacantan: Economy, Public Life, and Social Stratification. Stanford: Stanford University Press.

Carrasco, Pedro
1961 The Civil-Religious Hierarchy in Mesoamerican Communities: Pre-Spanish Background and Colonial Development. American Anthropologist 63:483–97.

Castro Pérez, Francisco
2006 Colapsos ambientales — transiciones culturales. Mexico City: UNAM / BUAP.

Chamoux, Marie-Noëlle
1992 Trabajo, técnicas y aprendizaje en el México indígena. Mexico City: CIESAS / CEMCA.

Chance, John K., and William B. Taylor
1985 Cofradías and cargos. American Ethnologist 12 (1): 1–26.

Cohen, Jeffrey
1999 Cooperation and Community: Society and Economy in Oaxaca. Austin: University of Texas Press.
2004 The Culture of Migration in Southern Mexico. Austin: University of Texas Press.

Collier, Jane F., and Silvia Yanagisako, eds.
1987 Gender and Kinship: Toward a Unified Analysis. Stanford: Stanford University Press.

DeWalt, Billie R.
1975 Changes in the Cargo Systems of Mesoamerica. Anthropological Quarterly 48:87–105.

Downing, T. E.
1973 Zapotec Inheritance. Ph.D. dissertation, Stanford University.

Durand, Jorge
1983 La ciudad invade al ejido. Mexico City: CIESAS (Ediciones de la Casa Chata).

Earle, Duncan
1986   The Metaphor of the Day in Quiché. *In* Symbol and Meaning beyond the
        Closed Community: Essays in Mesoamerican Ideas, edited by G. H. Gossen,
        155–72. Albany: Institute for Mesoamerican Studies, State University of New
        York at Albany.

Encarnación Ruiz, Junior Enrique
2004   La lucha entre dos Méxicos: La organización política y los conflictos con el
        estado de un pueblo situado en los límites de la expansiva zona metropoli-
        tana de la Ciudad de México. Master's thesis, Universidad Iberoamericana.

Ennis-McMillan, Michael
2001   La Purificación Tepetitla: Agua potable y cambio social en el somontano.
        Mexico City: Universidad Iberoamericana.

Fabian, Johannes
1983   Time and the Other: How Anthropology Makes Its Object. New York:
        Columbia University Press.

Foucault, Michel
1991   Governmentality. *In* The Foucault Effect: Studies in Governmentality,
        edited by G. Burchell, C. Gordon, and P. Miller, 87–104. London: Harvester
        Wheatsheaf.

Friedlander, Judith
1975   Being Indian in Hueyapan: A Study of Forced Identity in Contemporary
        Mexico. New York: St. Martin's Press.

Gamio, Manuel
1979 [1922]   La población del Valle de Teotihuacan. Mexico City: INI.

González de la Rocha, Mercedes
1994   The Resources of Poverty: Women and Survival in a Mexican City. Oxford,
        UK: Blackwell.

González Montes, S.
1992   Familias campesinas en el siglo XX. Doctoral dissertation, Universidad
        Complutense.

Good Eshelman, Catharine
2004a   La vida ceremonial en la construcción de la cultura: Procesos de identidad
        entre los nahuas de Guerrero. *In* Historia y vida ceremonial en las comuni-
        dades mesoamericanas: Los ritos agrícolas, edited by J. Broda and C. Good
        Eshelman, 127–49. Mexico City: INAH / UNAM.
2004b   Trabajando juntos: Los vivos, los muertos, la tierra y el maíz. *In* Historia y
        vida ceremonial en las comunidades mesoamericanas: Los ritos agrícolas,
        edited by J. Broda and C. Good Eshelman, 153–76. Mexico City: INAH /
        UNAM.
2005   "Trabajando juntos como uno": Conceptos nahuas del grupo doméstico
        y la persona. *In* Familia y parentesco en Mesoamérica: Unas miradas
        antropológicas, edited by D. Robichaux, 275–94. Mexico City: Universidad
        Iberoamericana.

Gossen, Gary H.
  1974   Chamulas in the World of the Sun. Cambridge, MA: Harvard University Press.
  1986   Mesoamerican Ideas as a Foundation for Regional Synthesis. *In* Symbol and Meaning beyond the Closed Community: Essays in Mesoamerican Ideas, edited by G. H. Gossen, 1–8. Albany: Institute for Mesoamerican Studies, State University of New York at Albany.
  1994   From Olmecs to Zapatistas: A Once and Future History of Souls. American Anthropologist 96 (3): 553–70.

Greenberg, James B.
  1981   Santiago's Sword: Chatino Peasant Religion and Economics. Berkeley: University of California Press.

Guiteras-Holmes, Calixta
  1961   Perils of the Soul: The World View of a Tzotzil Indian. Chicago: University of Chicago Press.

Hernández Castillo, Rosalía Aída
  2001   La otra frontera: Identidades múltiples en el Chiapas poscolonial. Mexico City: CIESAS / Porrúa.

Hill, Robert M., and John Monaghan
  1987   Continuities in Highland Maya Social Organization: Ethnohistory in Sacapulas, Guatemala. Philadelphia: University of Pennsylvania Press.

Hunt, Eva
  1977   The Transformation of the Hummingbird: Cultural Roots of a Zinacantecan Mythical Poem. Ithaca, NY: Cornell University Press.

Kearney, Michael
  1996   Reconceptualizing the Peasantry. Boulder, CO: Westview Press.

Klor de Alva, J. Jorge
  1997   Aztec Spirituality and Nahuatized Christianity. *In* South and Meso-american Native Spirituality: From the Cult of the Feathered Serpent to the Theology of Liberation, edited by G. H. Gossen, 173–97. New York: Crossroad Publishing Company.

Kuromiya, Aki
  2006   Salir adelante: Conflicto, armonía, y la práctica local del progreso en Santo Tomás Apipilhuasco, Estado de México. Master's thesis, Universidad Iberoamericana.
  2010   Las diferentes perspectivas y formas de progreso en Santo Tomás Apipilhuasco. *In* Texcoco en el nuevo milenio: Cambio y continuidad en una región periurbana del Valle de México, edited by R. Magazine and T. Martínez Saldaña, 273–93. Mexico City: Universidad Iberoamericana.

Kyle, Chris
  2008   Feeding Chilapa: The Birth, Life, and Death of a Mexican Region. Norman: University of Oklahoma Press.

Laughlin, Robert M.
  2010   First Steps. *In* Travelers to the Other World: A Maya View of North America, edited by C. Karasik, 23–55. Albuquerque: University of New Mexico Press.

Lechuga Paredes, Rubén Esteban
   2004   Tlaltecahuacan: Lugar de hombres con tierras divididas; Transformación y
          conflicto en un núcleo agrario. Master's thesis, Universidad Iberoamericana.

Lockhart, James
   1994   The Nahuas after the Conquest: A Social and Cultural History of the Indi-
          ans of Central Mexico, Sixteenth through Eighteenth Centuries. Stanford:
          Stanford University Press.

Lomnitz, Larissa Adler
   1977   Networks and Marginality: Life in a Mexican Shantytown. New York: Aca-
          demic Press.

López Austin, Alfredo
   1980   Cuerpo humano e ideología: Las concepciones de los antiguos nahuas.
          Mexico City: UNAM, IIA.
   2001   El núcleo duro, la cosmovisión y la tradición mesoamericana. In Cosmo-
          visión, ritual e identidad de los pueblos indígenas de México, edited by
          J. Broda and F. Báez-Jorge, 47–65. Mexico City: CONACULTA / Fondo de
          Cultura Económica.

López Millán, Minerva
   2008   "Sin ayuda no hay fiesta": Relaciones de reciprocidad en Santa Catarina del
          Monte. Ph.D. dissertation, Universidad Iberoamericana.

Maffie, James
   2003   To Walk in Balance: An Encounter between Contemporary Western Sci-
          ence and Conquest-Era Nahua Philosophy. In Science and Other Cultures:
          Issues in Philosophies of Science and Technology, edited by R. Figueroa and
          S. Harding, 70–90. New York: Routledge.

Magazine, Roger
   2003a Action, Personhood, and the Gift Economy among So-called Street Children
          in Mexico City. Social Anthropology 11 (3): 303–18.
   2003b An Innovative Combination of Neoliberalism and State Corporatism: The
          Case of a Locally Based NGO in Mexico City. Annals of the American Acad-
          emy of Political and Social Science 590:243–56.
   2004   Both Husbands and Banda (Gang) Members: Conceptualizing Marital Con-
          flict and Instability among Young Rural Migrants in Mexico City. Men and
          Masculinities 7 (2): 144–65.
   2010   De la ciudad al pueblo: Cambios en las prácticas laborales en el Acolhuacán
          neoliberal. In Texcoco en el nuevo milenio: Cambio y continuidad en una
          región periurbana del Valle de México, edited by R. Magazine and T. Mar-
          tínez Saldaña, 107–26. Mexico City: Universidad Iberoamericana.

Magazine, Roger, and Martha Areli Ramírez Sánchez
   2007   Continuity and Change in San Pedro Tlalcuapan, Mexico: Childhood,
          Social Reproduction, and Transnational Migration. In Generations and
          Globalization: Youth, Age, and Family in the New World Economy, edited
          by J. Cole and D. Durham, 52–73. Bloomington: Indiana University Press.

Malinowski, Bronislaw
   1926   Crime and Custom in Savage Society. London: Routledge and Kegan Paul.

Martin, Emily
    1994   Flexible Bodies: Tracking Immunity in American Culture from the Days of
            Polio to the Age of AIDS. Boston: Beacon Press.

Mathews, Holly F.
    1985   "We Are Mayordomo": A Reinterpretation of Women's Roles in the Mexican
            Cargo System. American Anthropologist 12 (2): 285–301.

Mauss, Marcel
    1990 [1923]   The Gift: The Form and Reason for Exchange in Archaic Societies.
            New York: W. W. Norton.

Medina Hernández, Andrés
    2007   Los pueblos originarios del sur del Distrito Federal: Una primera mirada
            etnográfica. *In* La memoria negada de la Ciudad de México: Sus pueblos
            originarios, edited by A. Medina Hernández, 29–124. Mexico City: UNAM /
            UACM.

Millán, Saúl
    2005   Los cargos en el sistema. *In* La organización social y ceremonial, edited by
            H. Topete Lara, L. Korsbaek, and M. M. Sepúlveda Garza, 217–38. Mexico
            City: ENAH / PROMEP-SEP.

Monaghan, John D.
    1990   Reciprocity, Redistribution, and the Transaction of Value in the Mesoameri-
            can fiesta. American Ethnologist 17 (4): 758–74.
    1995   The Covenants with Earth and Rain: Exchange, Sacrifice, and Revelation in
            Mixtec Sociality. Norman: University of Oklahoma Press.
    2008   Liturgical Forms of Economic Allocations. *In* Dimensions of Ritual Econ-
            omy, edited by E. C. Wells and P. A. McAnany, 19–35. Research in Eco-
            nomic Anthropology 27. Bingely, UK: Emerald Group Publishing.

Mulhare, Eileen M.
    2000   Mesoamerican Social Organization and Community after 1960. *In* Supple-
            ment to the Handbook of Middle American Indians, vol. 6, edited by J. D.
            Monaghan, 9–23. Austin: University of Texas Press.

Munn, Nancy
    1986   The Fame of Gawa: A Symbolic Study of Value Transformation in a Massim
            (Papua New Guinea) Society. Cambridge: Cambridge University Press.

Nash, Manning
    1958   Political Relations in Guatemala. Social and Economic Studies 7:65–75.

Neurath, Johannes
    2008   Alteridad constituyente y relaciones de tránsito en el ritual huichol: Ini-
            ciación, anti-iniciación y alianza. Cuicuilco 15 (42): 29–44.

Nutini, Hugo G.
    1968   San Bernardino Contla: Marriage and Family Structure in a Tlaxcalan Muni-
            cipio. Pittsburgh: University of Pittsburgh Press.
    1976   Introduction: The Nature and Treatment of Kinship in Mesoamerica. *In*
            Essays on Mexican Kinship, edited by H. G. Nutini, P. Carrasco, and J. M.
            Taggart, 3–27. Pittsburgh: University of Pittsburgh Press.

Nutini, Hugo G., Pedro Carrasco, and James M. Taggart, eds.
1976   Essays on Mexican Kinship. Pittsburgh: University of Pittsburgh Press.

Palerm, Ángel
1980   Antropología y Marxismo. Mexico City: Nueva Imagen.

Palerm, Ángel, and Eric Wolf
1972   Agricultura de riego en el viejo señorío de Acolhuacan. *In* Agricultura y civilización en Mesoamerica, 128–48. Mexico City: SEP.

Pérez Lizaur, Marisol
1977   Población y sociedad: Cuatro comunidades del Acolhuacan. Mexico City: CISINAH.

Pérez Lizaur, Marisol, and Scarlett Zamora Wasserman
2010   El mercado de ropa de Chiconcuac como detonador del desarrollo regional. *In* Texcoco en el nuevo milenio: Cambio y continuidad en una región periurbana del Valle de México, edited by R. Magazine and T. Martínez Saldaña, 55–82. Mexico City: Universidad Iberoamericana.

Pitarch, Pedro
2003a   Dos puntos de vista, una sola persona: El espacio en una montaña de almas. *In* Espacios mayas: Representaciones, usos, creencias, edited by A. Breton, A. M. Becquelin, and M. H. Ruz, 603–17. Mexico City: Centro de Estudios Mayas, IIFL, UNAM / CEMCA.
2003b   Infidelidades indígenas. Revista de Occidente, no. 270: 60–75.

Portal Ariosa, María Ana
1997   Ciudadanos desde el pueblo: Identidad urbana y religiosidad popular en San Andrés Totoltepec, Tlalpan, Mexico, D.F. Mexico City: Culturas Populares de México / UAM-Iztapalapa.

Povinelli, Elizabeth A.
2002   The Cunning of Recognition: Indigenous Alterities and the Making of Australian Multiculturalism. Durham, NC: Duke University Press.

Ramírez Sánchez, Martha Areli
2003   Ayudando en la casa: Ser niño de San Pedro Tlalcuapan; La construcción local de la infancia a través del trabajo en el ciclo doméstico. Master's thesis, Universidad Iberoamericana.

Redfield, Robert
1930   Tepoztlan, a Mexican village: A study in folk life. Chicago: University of Chicago Press.
1970 [1941]   The Folk Culture of the Yucatan. Chicago: University of Chicago Press.

Regehr, Vera
2005   "Estar juntos" y "Estar aparte" en San José Aztatla: Concepciones y prácticas locales del "grupo doméstico" en una comunidad mesoamericana. Master's thesis, Universidad Iberoamericana.

Robichaux, David
1997   Residence Rules and Ultimogeniture in Tlaxcala and Mesoamerica. Ethnology 36 (2): 149–71.

2005a ¿Dónde está el hogar? Retos metodológicos para el estudio del grupo doméstico en la Mesoamérica contemporánea. *In* Familia y parentesco en México y Mesoamérica: Unas miradas antropológicas, edited by D. Robichaux, 295–337. Mexico City: Universidad Iberoamericana.

2005b Introducción: La naturaleza y el tratamiento de la familia y el parentesco en México y Mesoamérica, treinta años después. *In* Familia y parentesco en México y Mesoamérica: Unas miradas antropológicas, edited by D. Robichaux, 29–97. Mexico City: Universidad Iberoamericana.

2005c Principios patrilineales en un sistema bilateral: Herencia y residencia y el sistema familiar mesoamericano. *In* Familia y parentesco en México y Mesoamérica: Unas miradas antropológicas, edited by D. Robichaux, 167–272. Mexico City: Universidad Iberoamericana.

2008 ¿De qué se trata el parentesco? Definiendo un objeto de estudio y algunas ideas para su investigación entre los nahuas y otros pueblos indígenas de Mesoamérica. Diario de campo. Suplemento No. 47. El mundo nahua: Parentesco y ritualidad (March–April): 65–82.

Robichaux, David, and Roger Magazine
2007 Las limitaciones de las categorías de "indígena" y "mestizo" en los estudios rurales de México. *In* El cambio en la sociedad rural mexicana: ¿Se valoran los recursos estratégos? Vol. 2, Pueblos indígenas, territorios y género en el México rural contemporáneo, edited by P. Sesia and S. Sarmiento, 190–209. Mexico City: AMER / Casa Juan Pablos / UAM / CONACyT / UAEM / Universidad Michoacana de San Nicolás de Hidalgo.

Rodríguez Hernández, Dula Celina
2008 Las mayordomías en Chiconcuac, Estado de México. Familia y parentesco en la organización de las fiestas patronales. Master's thesis, Universidad Iberoamericana.

Rothstein, Frances Abrahamer
1982 Three Different Worlds: Women, Men and Children in an Industrializing Community. Westport, CT: Greenwood Press.

2007 Globalization in Rural Mexico: Three Decades of Change. Austin: University of Texas Press.

Rouse, Roger
1992 Making Sense of Settlement: Class Transformation, Cultural Struggle, and Transnationalism among Mexican Migrants in the United States. *In* Towards a Transnational Perspective on Migration: Race, Class, Ethnicity, and Nationalism Reconsidered, edited by N. Glick Schiller, L. Basch, and C. Blanc-Szanton, 25–52. Annals of the New York Academy of Sciences 645. New York: New York Academy of Sciences.

Rus, Jan, and Robert Wasserstrom
1980 Civil-Religious Hierarchies in Central Chiapas: A Critical Perspective. American Anthropologist 7 (3): 466–78.

Sandstrom, Alan R.
1991 Corn Is Our Blood: Culture and Ethnic Identity in a Contemporary Aztec Indian Village. Norman: University of Oklahoma Press.

Schneider, David M.
  1980 [1968]   American Kinship: A Cultural Account. Chicago: University of Chicago Press.
  1984   A Critique of the Study of Kinship. Ann Arbor: University of Michigan Press.

Severi, Carlo
  2004   Capturing Imagination: A Cognitive Approach to Cultural Complexity. Journal of the Royal Anthropological Institute 10:815–38.

Simmel, Georg
  1978 [1907]   The Philosophy of Money. London: Routledge and Kegan Paul.
  2000   The Metropolis and Mental Life. *In* Simmel on Culture: Selected Writings. Edited by David Frisby and Mike Featherstone, 174–85. London: Sage.

Slade, Doren
  1992   Making the World Safe for Existence: Celebration of the Saints among the Sierra Nahuat of Chignautla, Mexico. Ann Arbor: University of Michigan Press.

Smith, Waldemar R.
  1977   The Fiesta System and Economic Change. New York: Columbia University Press.

Sokolovsky, Jay
  2010   La respuesta social y económica a la globalización en una comunidad indígena de la sierra texcocana. *In* Texcoco en el nuevo milenio: Cambio y continuidad en una región periurbana del Valle de México, edited by R. Magazine and T. Martínez Saldaña, 33–53. Mexico City: Universidad Iberoamericana.

Speed, Shannon
  2007   Rights in Rebellion: Indigenous Struggle and Human Rights in Chiapas. Stanford: Stanford University Press.

Speed, Shannon, Rosalía Aída Hernández Castillo, and Lynn Stephen, eds.
  2006   Dissident Women: Gender and Cultural Politics in Chiapas. Austin: University of Texas Press.

Stephen, Lynn
  1991   Zapotec Women. Austin: University of Texas Press.
  2002   Zapata Lives! Histories and Cultural Politics in Southern Mexico. Berkeley: University of California Press.

Strathern, Marilyn
  1988   The Gender of the Gift: Problems with Women and Problems with Society in Melanesia. Berkeley: University of California Press.
  1992   After Nature: English Kinship in the Late Twentieth Century. Cambridge: Cambridge University Press.

Taggart, James M.
  1991 [1975]   Estructura de los grupos domésticos de una comunidad de habla náhuatl de Puebla. Mexico City: INI.
  1997 [1983]   Nahuat Myth and Social Structure. Austin: University of Texas Press.

2007   Remembering Victoria: A Tragic Nahuat Love Story. Austin: University of Texas Press.

Trouillot, Michel-Rolph
  1991   Anthropology and the Savage Slot: The Poetics and Politics of Otherness. *In* Recapturing Anthropology: Working in the Present, edited by R. G. Fox, 17–44. Santa Fe, NM: School of American Research Press.

Velásquez Velásquez, Ángela María
  2007   Ayudar, participar y convivir: Jóvenes, familia y comunidad en San Juan Tezontla, Estado de México. Master's thesis, Universidad Iberoamericana.

Vilaça, Aparecida
  2010   Strange Enemies: Indigenous Agency and Scenes of Encounters in Amazonia. Durham, NC: Duke University Press.

Viveiros de Castro, Eduardo
  1998   Cosmological Deixis and Amerindian Perspectivism. Journal of the Royal Anthropological Institute 4 (3): 469–88.
  2004   Exchanging Perspectives: The Transformation of Objects into Subjects in Amerindian Ontologies. Common Knowledge 10 (3): 463–84.

Vogt, Evon
  1969   Zinacantan: A Maya Community in the Highlands of Chiapas. Cambridge, MA: Harvard University Press.
  1976   Tortillas for the Gods: A Symbolic Analysis of Zinacanteco Ritual. Cambridge, MA: Harvard University Press.

Wagner, Roy
  1981 [1975]   The Invention of Culture. Chicago: University of Chicago Press.

Warman, Arturo
  1980   Ensayos sobre el campesinado en México. Mexico City: Nueva Imagen.

Wolf, Eric R.
  1955   The Types of Latin American Peasantry. American Anthropologist 57 (3): 452–71.

Yanagisako, Silvia
  1979   Family and Household: The Analysis of Domestic Groups. Annual Review of Anthropology 8:161–205.

Index

About the Author

Roger Magazine has held the position of professor in the Graduate Program in Social Anthropology at the Universidad Iberoamericana in Mexico City since 1999. He received his PhD in anthropology from The Johns Hopkins University in 2000 and is currently a member of Mexico's National System of Researchers, level two. He is the author of the book *Golden and Blue Like My Heart: Masculinity, Youth, and Power Among Soccer Fans in Mexico City* (University of Arizona Press, 2007) and co-editor of the volumes *Texcoco en el nuevo milenio: Cambio y continuidad en una región periurbana del Valle de México* (Universidad Iberoamericana, 2010) and *Afición futbolística y rivalidades en el México contemporáneo: Una mirada nacional* (Universidad Iberoamericana, 2012).